MARCO POLO AND HIS WORLD

Covering one of the most fascinating yet misunderstood periods in history, the MEDIEVAL LIVES series presents medieval people, concepts and events, drawing on political and social history, philosophy, material culture (art, architecture and archaeology) and the history of science. These books are global and wide-ranging in scope, encompassing both Western and non-Western subjects, and span the fifth to the fifteenth centuries, tracing significant developments from the collapse of the Roman Empire onwards.

SERIES EDITOR: Deirdre Jackson

MARCO POLO AND HIS WORLD

SHARON KINOSHITA

REAKTION BOOKS

For Will

Published by Reaktion Books Ltd
Unit 32, Waterside
44–48 Wharf Road
London N1 7UX, UK
www.reaktionbooks.co.uk

First published 2024
Copyright © Sharon Kinoshita 2024

Printed and bound in India by Replika Press Pvt. Ltd

A catalogue record for this book is available from the British Library

ISBN 978 1 78914 937 1

CONTENTS

世祖
皇帝
后

微伯尼

1 Anige, *Chabi*, 1294, album leaf, ink and colours on silk.

Introduction

At first glance, one could scarcely imagine a better candidate for a series on medieval lives than Marco Polo (1254–1324). Few figures from the European Middle Ages have greater name recognition today. This is all the more remarkable since he was neither a king, like Charlemagne or William the Conqueror; nor a holy figure, like St Francis of Assisi or Joan of Arc; nor a literary giant, like Dante or Chaucer. Rather, he came from a family of Venetian merchants who lived at an extraordinary moment when the Mongol conquests of Chinggis Khan and his descendants had created the conditions for trans-Asian communication and exchange on a scale unprecedented in world history. Leaving home at age seventeen in the company of his father, Niccolò, and his uncle, Maffeo, Marco travelled to the court of the Great Khan Qubilai (Chinggis's grandson), whose favour the elder Polos had earned on a previous visit, when Marco was still a boy. Attracting Qubilai's attention through his gift for languages and his knack for recounting captivating tales about far-flung places, Marco spent his twenties and thirties in the service of the Great Khan. Finally, in the early 1290s, the three Polos were included in Qubilai's embassy to his great-nephew, the Ilkhan of Persia. From there, they made their way back home, reaching Venice in 1295, some 24 years after Marco, now aged about 41, had originally left.

We have little record of Marco's activities immediately following his return. By 1298, however, he found himself a prisoner in Genoa, Venice's great commercial rival in the eastern Mediterranean, the Black Sea and Western Asia. There he met a fellow prisoner from Pisa, another of Genoa's fierce maritime competitors: Rustichello, a writer of Arthurian romances skilled in composing long narratives in French. Together, the two produced a book on 'the diverse parts of the world and its great marvels' that Marco had come to know, through direct experience or through reliable hearsay, while traversing Asia over the preceding two and a half decades. The result was the work commonly known today as Marco Polo's *Travels*. Its original title, however, was *The Description of the World* (*Le Devisement du monde*) – the first of several names under which it was known in the Middle Ages and beyond.

The Man

In contrast to contemporaries like the great Florentine poet Dante Alighieri (1265–1321), Marco Polo leaves surprisingly little trace in the historical record. Behind the many attempts to romanticize his life, what little we know about the Polos comes from a handful of documents drafted during Marco's lifetime by various members of the family.[1] A will drawn up by his uncle, an elder Marco, in 1280 disposed of his share of a partnership with Niccolò and Maffeo near the midpoint of their time in Asia. Though this property included buildings in the parish of San Severo in Venice and in the Crimean port of Soldaia, the sums divided among his heirs were modest. After the three Polos returned to Venice in 1295, however, the family's fortune increased considerably; in particular, they seem to have traded heavily in musk, the exotic animal-derived substance prized in medieval perfumery, in which Marco showed a special interest. By 1300, the Polos held considerable property in the Venetian parish of San Giovanni Grisostomo, across the Grand Canal and slightly upstream from the great marketplace at the Rialto. A sure sign of the family's enhanced status was Marco's marriage to Donata Badoer, from one of Venice's pre-eminent families; the couple's three daughters, Fantina, Bellela and Moreta, would likewise marry into the city's social and economic elite. When Marco died in 1324, his personal fortune (augmented by inheritances from his father, his brother and his uncle Maffeo) amounted to an estate worth over 10,000 gold ducats; the annual allowance he left to his widow Donata was four times greater than the average. Among the possessions inventoried at his death were 24 beds, indicating a large household (probably including a number of domestic slaves, not uncommon in Italy and across the medieval world); numerous items of clothing; and pieces of cloth, including silks of different grade, pattern, colour and origin. Also listed were mementos of his time among the Mongols: a golden *paiza* – one of the four 'tablets of command' given to the Polos by Qubilai's great-nephew Geikhatu on their homeward journey to assure their safe passage through the Ilkhanate of Persia (*Description of the World* §19, p. 13; references hereafter refer to this text) – and a *boqta,* the distinctive formal headdress worn by elite Mongol women (illus. 1). Together, these items help fill out the picture of the life of a prosperous Venetian merchant with long experience in Asia. Anything further about Marco Polo must be deduced from the *Description of the World* itself.

The Book

The original work composed by Marco Polo and Rustichello of Pisa in 1298 has been lost. The closest surviving copy, known as the 'F' text, comes down to us in a modest manuscript copied

2 Marco Polo, *Le Devisement du monde*, 14th century, last page of the table of contents and first page of text.

circa 1310 and today housed in Paris in the Bibliothèque nationale de France (illus. 2). Like the presumed lost original, this
'F' text was composed not in Italian (as the 'nationality' of its
co-authors might lead us to suppose) but in an Italianate French
known to scholars today as Franco-Italian. In this generation
before the Florentine poet Dante Alighieri's *Divine Comedy*
raised the Tuscan dialect to the dignity of a literary language,
French (the vernacular shared by much of Latin Europe's secular elite) was the language of choice for non-clerical Italians
wishing to reach an audience not highly schooled in Latin. As
Marco's compatriot Martin da Canal explained in his *History
of Venice* (*Les Estoires de Venise*), composed in 1267, 'the French
language has spread all over the world, and is the most delightful
to read and hear above any other.'[2]

The *Description of the World*, as it survives in the Franco-
Italian 'F' text, consists of 233 chapters, varying in length from
a few short lines to several pages in the modern printed edition.
It falls into four main parts: a prologue (§§1–19), narrating the
Polos' two journeys to the court of Qubilai Khan, who ruled the
Mongol Empire from 1260 to 1294 – the first journey made by
Marco's father and uncle in the 1260s and the second made by
the trio between 1271 and 1295; 'the book' proper (§§20–157),
devoted in the main to the vast territories under Mongol rule;
the 'Book of India' (§§158–198), describing the lands bordering
the 'Ocean Sea', beginning with Japan and sweeping down
through peninsular and insular Southeast Asia to the coastal
regions of India, then across the Indian Ocean to the east coast
of Africa; and a coda (§§199–233), ostensibly on 'Greater Turkey'
but mainly recounting histories of the conflict within and between
the Mongol khanates ruled by various branches of Chinggis
Khan's descendants.[3]

Across these 233 chapters, Marco's account includes many
diverse narrative types. Most numerous by far are the entries

devoted to specific cities, provinces or kingdoms. In their most schematic form, these typically list the inhabitants' religion, their political allegiance or form of rule, their source of livelihood (trade, crafts, agriculture), and any commodities of particular interest to merchants. The entry on the northern Chinese city of Hezhongfu (in modern Shanxi province) is typical: 'The people are idolators and burn their dead. They belong to the Great Khan and have notes for currency. They live from trade and crafts. They have a lot of gold and silk and *sendal* in great abundance. This city has many cities and castles under its rule' (§131, p. 117). Longer entries might include proto-ethnographic accounts of noteworthy cultural features (dress, customs, food), recent history (especially how the place in question came under Mongol rule), or marvels, including miracle stories, associated with local sites or figures. Along the way, Marco shows consistent interest in matters related to commerce: whether merchants are well- or ill-treated; the infrastructure (markets, special districts, warehouses and transport systems, including roads, navigable waterways and bridges) available to facilitate trade; and the volume and quality of particular commodities (pearls or pepper or silks) to be had in one location or another. Charmingly, Marco at times waxes enthusiastic in describing a region's animal life, even where it has no bearing on trade.

This variety of topics and styles makes it impossible to assign the book to any one genre; scholars have noticed resemblances to the merchant's manual, the wonder book, the crusading tract, the missionary manual, the chronicle and the encyclopaedia, as well as Old French epic and romance. A central focus of the *Description*, however, is Qubilai Khan, 'the most powerful [ruler] in men, land, and treasure that the world has ever seen' (§76, p. 67), and his vast empire. Marco begins his account of the Mongols with a detailed history of Chinggis Khan's rise to power (§§65–8). Then, quickly passing over the intervening reigns, he comes to Qubilai: his early campaigns as Great Khan (khagan), his family, his palace, his court and its festivities and peregrinations, the social and infrastructural improvements he has brought to the land and its people. For Marco, Qubilai's greatness is singular, not to be compared to that of any man, 'from Adam our first father until now' (§76, p. 67). This unprecedented portrait – stunning to an audience accustomed to citing figures like Alexander, Caesar or Charlemagne as standards of political power – goes a long way in accounting for the title soon given to some Old French versions of Marco's text, *The Book of the Great Khan*.

Afterlives

This emphasis on Qubilai and his empire makes it easy to understand the variant title *The Book of the Great Khan* given to Marco's text in some subsequent French manuscripts. In the century and more following its original composition, Marco Polo's *Description of the World* was invested with different meanings through translation, through scribal additions or abridgements, through the illuminations accompanying it, and through the other texts with which it was copied or bound. In the decade or so after the Franco-Italian 'F' text was produced, the Dominican friar Francesco Pipino translated and reworked a version of Marco's text into Latin under the title *On the Conditions and Customs of Eastern Regions* (*De conditionibus et consuetudinibus orientalium regionum*). In the mid-1330s a French copy called *The Book of the Great Khan* (*Li livres du Grant Caam*) appeared in a lavish manuscript made for the French king Philip VI (London, British Library, Royal MS 19 D I) (illus. 3). In the first decade of the fifteenth century, another manuscript, today housed in the University of Oxford's Bodleian Library, added a close copy of the text of the British Library version and a Middle English poem

3 The elder Polos meeting Qubilai Khan, miniature from Marco Polo,
Li livres du Grant Caam, 1333–c. 1340.

on an episode in the life of Alexander the Great to a copy of the
Romance of Alexander dating from more than fifty years before;
the images, though placed identically to those in the British
Library manuscript, compositionally and stylistically parallel
those in the *Romance of Alexander*, bringing the two texts into
close visual as well as thematic alignment (illus. 4).

At about the same time (*c.* 1410), Marco's work was included
in a richly illustrated compilation of texts about Asia that the
Duke of Burgundy commissioned as a New Year's gift for his
uncle, the famous bibliophile John, Duke of Berry. Today housed
in Paris (BNF MS Français 2810), it bears the title *The Book of
Marvels* (*Le Livre des merveilles*) (illus. 5).

Beyond differences in textual detail and presentation, each of these subsequent copies of Marco Polo's book was produced in a distinct historical context that would have shaped its meaning and reception. Most notably, the Yuan dynasty, founded by Qubilai Khan in 1271, was overthrown in China by the Ming dynasty in 1368 (the Ilkhanids having been overthrown in Persia over three decades before). Latin Europeans would have had a hazy, if any, knowledge of these world-historical changes. Then, at the turn of the fifteenth century, another conqueror sweeping westward from Central Asia reached the shores of the Mediterranean: Timur the Lame (later immortalized by Shakespeare's contemporary Christopher Marlowe as Tamburlaine), self-proclaimed successor to the Mongol khans, whose defeat and capture of the sultan Bayezid at the Battle of Ankara in 1402 threw the Ottoman Empire into disarray for more than a decade. By the last quarter of the fifteenth century the impulse to exploration and expansion that would lead to Columbus's voyage to the New World in 1492 and Vasco da Gama's to India in 1498 brought renewed interest in Marco's text, marked by the publication of several print editions beginning in 1477.

In the context of the early modern age of exploration, Marco's text was reconfigured as a travel narrative. In 1532 it appeared in *Novus Orbis*, a Latin collection of mostly contemporary maps and seventeen travel narratives. This volume proved highly influential: it was quickly translated into German (1534) and Flemish (1536), and the version of Marco's text it contained, under the title 'Of Eastern Lands' (*De Regionibus orientalibus*), was translated separately into various vernacular languages, becoming the sixteenth century's most widespread version of the *Description*. Then in 1559 – now well into the age of European exploration and conquest – the Venetian humanist Giovanni Battista Ramusio published an Italian print translation.

4 The Polos leaving Venice, miniature from Marco Polo, *Li livres du Grant Caam*, 1338–1410.

5 Dog-headed men, miniature from Marco Polo, *Le Livre des merveilles*, 1400–1420.

Appearing in his series 'On Navigations and Travels' (*Delle navigationi et viaggi*), it contained many passages not found in previous versions.

   This early modern publication history undoubtedly helped seal our modern pigeonholing of Marco's text as a quintessential travel narrative. Yet when we return to the 'F' text – the version of Marco and Rustichello's book widely acknowledged to be closest to the lost original – what we find is not a travel narrative at all. As we have seen, only the first 19 of its 233 chapters recount the direct experience, first of Niccolò and Maffeo, then of the two elder Polos together with Marco. Readers expecting to find a first-person account of heroic journeys, unique encounters and the travails of the road are bound to be disappointed. Similarly, efforts to map the sites Marco describes as a single linear itinerary are likely to result in conclusions of his confusion or faulty memory. This in turn contributes to scepticism about the 'truth' of his account: *Did Marco Polo go to China?* Sinologist Frances Wood asked this in a book whose title strongly suggested that he did not. (This challenge was powerfully refuted by a number of experts on China, and in the afterword to the American edition of her book Wood herself walked back the claim – which, she explains, was the result of having consulted 'modern versions of the text, cobbled together from a great variety of versions'.[4])

   If, however, we take Marco and Rustichello at their word and read their book as a 'description of the world', something quite different appears. We discover instead a multitude – or, to use their word, 'diversity' – of places that Marco may have visited and revisited over his two-decade stay, lived in for months or years at a time, traversed once on his outward and homebound journeys, learned about from administrative records or from the reports of 'authoritative men of truth' (§1, p. 1) such as he would have frequented in Mongol service. This is the world, recounted in ways calculated to astonish Marco's contemporaries, that the present volume seeks to bring to life.

Marco Polo Describes His World

Perhaps anomalously, given how well known Marco Polo remains today, this book focuses not on the explorer's life; rather, we take his and Rustichello of Pisa's *Description of the World* as a window onto the remarkable half-century between circa 1250 and 1300, when the Mongol conquest of Asia enabled unprecedented commerce, contact and communication between lands stretching from the Mediterranean in the west to the Pacific Ocean in the east and the Indian Ocean to the south. Chapter One sets the stage, exploring the way that world-historical events like the fall of Baghdad (1258), the Byzantine reconquest of Constantinople (1261) and the loss of the crusader city of Acre (1291) helped to shape not only the geopolitics but the commerce and culture of this distinctive period. Chapters Two and Three use the *Description*'s two later medieval titles – *The Book of the Great Khan* and *The Book of Marvels*, respectively – to bring different aspects of the text into focus. Chapter Two focuses on the grandeur of Qubilai and his empire as seen through Marco Polo's eyes, while Chapter Three examines the *Description*'s particular refashioning of the medieval fascination for wonders (*merveilles* in French, *mirabilia* in Latin and *ajā'ib* in Arabic), from prodigies of nature to miracle stories (retold in ways that depart from Latin Christian traditions) to curiosities of culture. Chapters Four and Five move out into the world beyond the text. The former looks at the various commodities traded across Eurasia – those animal, vegetable and mineral products that drew the Polos and other European merchants eastward in the first place. The latter – the most experimental part of this book – takes up the challenge of exploring the cultural richness of Marco Polo's world by looking at the lives of three individuals, Marco's exact contemporaries, whose stories illuminate its variety and brilliance: the Chinese painter and *literatus* Zhao Mengfu, the Delhi poet Amīr Khusrau and the Byzantine princess and khatun of Persia Maria Palaiologina.

ONE

Marco Polo and His World

Lords, emperors and kings, dukes and marquises, counts,
knights and townsfolk, and all of you who wish to know the
diverse races of men and the *diversities* of the *diverse* regions of
the world, take this book and have it read. Here you will find
all the greatest marvels and great *diversities* of Greater Armenia,
Persia, the Tartars, India, and many other provinces, as our book
will tell you clearly, in orderly fashion, just as Messer Marco
Polo, wise and noble citizen of Venice, tells because he saw it
with his own eyes.
§1, p. 1, emphases added

These are the opening lines of Marco Polo and Rustichello
of Pisa's *Description of the World*, inaugurating a textual
tradition characterized by diversity: of languages (being
translated and retranslated into standard Old French, Latin,
Tuscan, Venetian and a spate of other European languages); of
manuscripts (no two versions being the same) and of titles.
Thus it is striking that Rustichello's prologue begins with four
iterations of the adjective 'diverse' or the noun 'diversity'. Such
ungainly repetition, so grating on modern ears, is simply an exag-
gerated version of a stylistic trait widespread in thirteenth-century
French, as in the great Arthurian prose romances *The Quest of
the Holy Grail* (*La Queste del saint graal*) or *The Death of King
Arthur* (*La Mort le roi Artu*). English translations typically

conceal this stylistic clunkiness under a more varied vocabulary, rendering the text more elegant but at the price of erasing one of Marco and Rustichello's greatest thematic emphases.[1]

This repetition is not the only way the prologue registers their focus on diversity. Its opening invocation, which has attracted critical attention for its close resemblance to the first line of Rustichello of Pisa's own Arthurian romance *Méliadus*, calls out to a remarkably wide audience. Two previous 'reports' on the Mongols, composed in Latin by the Franciscan friars John of Plano Carpini in the 1240s and William of Rubruck in the 1250s, were addressed to Pope Innocent IV and King Louis IX of France, respectively; vernacular literary texts in Old French commonly invoked the noble or royal patron who had commissioned them or whose favour their authors sought to attract. Rustichello, in contrast, casts an exceedingly wide net, beginning with imperial, royal and noble listeners at the very top of the secular social order, but descending quickly to 'knights and townsfolk' before finally throwing open the gates to anyone who wishes to hear of the diversity of the world. Conspicuously absent are clerics of any kind, from the pope on downwards through the hierarchy, who would receive their own customized version in Fra Francesco Pipino's Latin translation. Rustichello's prologue, in sum, represents an audacious act of social imagining, assembling a virtual readership unthinkable in any face-to-face gathering. Perhaps it is not a stretch to attribute the diversity of discourses found in the pages of the *Description* (which we will explore shortly) to this diversity of audience.

A second point to note in these lines is Rustichello's summary of the book's contents: 'all the greatest marvels and great diversities of Greater Armenia, Persia, the Tartars, India, and many other provinces.' ('Tartar' – derived from the ethnic or tribal designation Tatar, inflected by 'Tartarus', the ancient Greek name for the underworld, is the term consistently used for the

De afia & partib' ei.

asia

evropa   affrica

6a   des

6 Diagrammatic T-O map, drawing from Isidore of Seville, *Etymologiae*, early 13th century.

Mongols throughout the *Description* and other Latin European writings.) Conspicuously absent is any division of the world into 'East' and 'West', ubiquitous in modern studies of Marco Polo. Also missing are references to the three continents, familiar from medieval T-O maps – so-called from the 'O' formed by the great encircling Ocean and the 'T' of the three waterways trisecting the world's land mass (illus. 6). Brunetto Latini's encyclopaedic compilation *The Book of the Treasure* (*Li livres dou trésor*), composed in French in the 1260s, reflects this conventional medieval vision of the world:

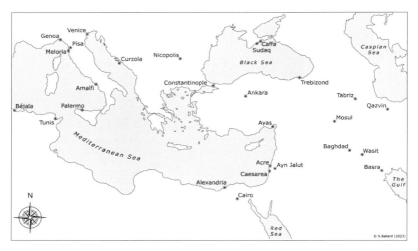

7 Map of the medieval Mediterranean.

> The earth is girded and surrounded by . . . the great sea,
> which is called the Ocean, and all the other seas which
> flow throughout different parts of the earth are extensions
> of it . . . all the earth is divided into three parts: Asia,
> Africa, and Europe. But this is not accurate, for Asia
> contains half of the whole earth.[2]

Most strikingly, the prologue makes no mention of China
– the land most closely associated with Marco Polo in the modern
imagination. Rather, Rustichello offers us an accumulation of
geo-cultural entities – 'Greater Armenia, Persia, the Tartars,
India, and many other provinces': an expandable frame that
highlights the multiplicity and diversity of the thirteenth-
century world.

A Tale of Three Cities

We begin close to home. Today, Venice, Pisa and Genoa are three stops on the tourist circuit of Italy, famous for their historical sites or as ports of call for Mediterranean cruises. In Marco Polo's day, however, all three were autonomous maritime republics (along with Amalfi, whose heyday had come two centuries earlier) and bitter trade rivals. In fact, while municipal officials typically made much of their crusading efforts against Muslim powers on the southern and eastern shores of the Mediterranean, they often saved their most intense animus for their fellow Christian commercial competitors (illus. 7). In his *Chronicle of the City of Genoa*, Archbishop Jacopo da Varagine compared his city's naval victory over the Venetians in a battle fought in 1294 near Ayas (in Cilician Armenia) to the victory of the Maccabees, vastly outnumbered, in their revolt against Seleucid Persia. Furthermore, Jacopo relates, the Venetians compounded the shame of their defeat by attempting to 'whitewash' the account of their humiliation at sea with 'certain colorful fictions'.[3] Such trenchant realpolitik, from the pen of a cleric best known to modern scholars for his anthology of saints' lives, *The Golden Legend* (*Legenda Aurea*), provides vivid context for how it was that Marco, the Venetian, and Rustichello, the Pisan, found themselves together in Genoese captivity in 1298.

Venice

In 1267 Marco's compatriot Martin da Canal composed a history of Venice, *Les Estoires de Venise* – in French, like the *Description of the World* – in order to highlight the glories of the city. After his pious invocations of 'Our Lord Jesus Christ', 'Our Lady Holy Mary' and 'the beloved evangelist Monseignor Saint Mark' (Venice's patron saint), he turns to the city itself:

the most attractive and pleasant of our age, filled with
beauty and all good things; merchandise flows through this
noble city like water through fountains. Venice rises out
of the sea, and salt water runs through it and around every
place except in the houses and the streets. And when the
citizens are in the public squares, they can return to their
houses either by land or by water.

This focus on water of course captures the distinctiveness of
Venice, built across myriad islands in the Venetian Lagoon – a
patchwork of parishes each with its own church, *campo* (market
square) and *palazzi* (grand residences) of its leading families,
connected by ferries and wooden bridges. The flow of water,
however, is introduced not for its own sake but as a simile. As
Martin elaborates:

Commercial goods come from everywhere, along with
merchants who buy the products they desire, which they
then take back to their own countries. In this city, one
can find an enormous amount of food, bread and wine,
fowl and water birds, fresh and salted meats, and great fish
from the sea or from the river; there are merchants from
everywhere who come to buy and sell.

Abundance is marked not by spiritual riches but by the diversity
of foodstuffs. Even the well-born nobles who would hold pride
of place in other civic descriptions are nearly squeezed out by
the attention given to merchants, craftsmen and sailors.

In this beautiful city there are a great number of
gentlemen, including the old, the middle-aged, and
the young, the nobility of whose birth warrants great
praise; with them, merchants who buy and sell, money

changers and citizens practicing every craft, mariners of all sorts and boats that transport them to any locale, and warships used to cause injury to the enemy. Also in this city there are many beautiful ladies, maidens, and girls, in abundance, very richly clothed.[4]

As in Rustichello of Pisa's prologue, clerics are again conspicuous by their absence.

Founded in the fifth century by refugees fleeing barbarian incursions, Venice developed from settlements across the myriad islands of the lagoon at a time when the Byzantine Empire stood as the undisputed centre of the Christian world. Although far enough from Constantinople to enjoy relative autonomy, it remained turned towards the eastern Mediterranean. A pivotal moment came in 828 when, according to tradition, Venetian merchants trading in Alexandria stole the relics of St Mark the Evangelist, an example of the medieval practice of 'holy theft' (*furtum sacrum*), and brought them back to Venice, where the first church of St Mark was built (on the site of the present basilica) to house them. A second turning point for Venice, as for the other Italian maritime republics, came in the wake of the success of the First Crusade (1099). Having supported the war effort with logistics – transportation and supplies – as well as fighting, the Venetians were rewarded with 'quarters' (neighbourhoods) and trade privileges in the newly founded kingdom of Jerusalem and the other crusader states. These settlements led to the expansion of trade with Alexandria, the great emporium for spices and other commodities coming via the maritime route from South Asia and the East Indies as well as for local or regional products like sugar and alum. In 1173 the great Muslim leader Saladin had granted the Venetians a *fondaco* – a complex for foreign merchants modelled on the Islamic institution of the *funduq* – comprising lodgings, warehouses and

8 Horses (replicas), bronze, Basilica of San Marco, Venice.

other facilities, including (in the case of visiting Christians) a church.[5]

Venice's power and prosperity took a significant leap at the beginning of the thirteenth century. In 1204, at the instigation of the aged doge Enrico Dandolo (then in his nineties), the forces of the Fourth Crusade, originally mustered to attack Ayyubid Egypt, instead conquered the eastern Christian city of Constantinople, capital of the Byzantine Empire. Famously, some of Venice's most iconic objects came to the city as spoils of this conquest: the horses of San Marco, from Constantine's hippo-drome, today mounted (in replica) high above the main facade of the basilica (illus. 8); the two pairs of porphyry statues (often called the Four Tetrarchs) hugging the southwest corner of the basilica at ground level (illus. 9); and the so-called Pillars of Acre (*Pilastri Acritani*) outside its southern face – long thought to have been taken from the crusader port of Acre after a battle with

9 Four Tetrarchs, c. 300 CE, porphyry, Basilica of San Marco, Venice.

the Genoese but recently revealed to have come from the sixth-century church of St Polyeuktos in Constantinople (illus. 10).

More significantly, Venice's alliance with the newly installed 'Latin' emperors (descendants of the counts of Flanders) gave it major trading privileges in the city and control over access to the Black Sea; in addition, it claimed as its territorial gains a string of ports – the island of Crete, Negroponte (modern Euboea) in the Aegean Sea and Modon and Coron (modern Koroni and Methoni, respectively) in the Ionian – to serve as stepping stones for maritime transit across the eastern Mediterranean, thus helping to consolidate the republic's overseas dominions, the so-called *Stato da Mar*. This expansive Venetian network provides the context for the elder Polos' first voyage (§2) in 1260, when they set out from Constantinople for the Crimean port of Sudaq (near modern Feodosia). Fortunes changed again, however, in the following year when Michael VIII Palaiologos, descendant of a former Byzantine imperial line and ruler of the rump state of Nicaea, ousted the Latin emperor and his Venetian supporters. Now it was the turn of his allies, the

10 *Pilastri Acritani*, 6th century CE, Basilica of San Marco, Venice.

Genoese, to benefit from the advantages that trading privileges in Constantinople could confer – a significant reversal of political and economic fortunes between the two greatest trading powers of the high medieval Mediterranean. This, then, was the situation during Marco Polo's boyhood, in the decade in which his father, Niccolò, and uncle Maffeo were away on their first journey into Asia.

As with most cities, the built environment of modern Venice represents a layering of centuries, periods and styles. Many of the sites admired by today's tourists post-date Marco Polo's lifetime: both the Doge's Palace, adjacent to St Mark's Basilica, and the splendid Veneto-Gothic mansions (*palazzi*) lining the Grand Canal assumed their present aspect between the fourteenth and fifteenth centuries. The Franciscan church of Santa Maria Gloriosa dei Frari and the Dominican basilica of Santi Giovanni e Paolo were both built in the 1330s, replacing humbler thirteenth-century structures – a reflection of the rapid growth and influence of these two great mendicant orders. The Rialto Bridge, one of the city's most recognizable monuments, was not built in stone until the end of the sixteenth century – contemporary with Shakespeare's *Merchant of Venice* with its famous line, 'What news on the Rialto?' (III.1).

Nevertheless, Venice did undergo considerable change during Marco Polo's lifetime. The basic structure of the Venetian *palazzo* – storerooms on the ground floor, *salone* (central hall) and living quarters on the second floor – took shape in the second half of the thirteenth century. Under the doges Ranieri Zeno (1253–68) and Lorenzo Tiepolo (1268–75), Venice must have seemed very much a city under construction. In 1264 a wooden drawbridge replaced the twelfth-century pontoon bridge spanning the Grand Canal at the Rialto (central market), and the Merceria, the street connecting the Rialto to San Marco, was paved in 1272.

11 Gentile Bellini, *Procession in Piazza San Marco* (detail), tempera and oil on canvas, 1496.

At the heart of these urban transformations was the basilica of San Marco. Unlike the other great churches of medieval Latin Europe, it was not a cathedral but, despite its grand proportions, the private chapel of the doge. And in contrast to those monuments built in the styles we today call Romanesque and Gothic, its domes (said to be modelled after those of the Church of the Holy Apostles in Constantinople) and its mosaics conspicuously proclaimed Venice's link to its Byzantine past. After the Fourth Crusade, as noted above, the facade of the basilica was transformed by the spolia brought back from Constantinople. Celebrating a city's triumphs and promoting its greatness through the ostentatious display of material objects was common to all three of our maritime republics but nowhere was it done more spectacularly than in Venice. In 1261, as we have seen, Venetian commerce suffered a major setback when the Byzantine reconquest of Constantinople delivered the trade privileges its merchants had previously enjoyed into the hands of their rivals, the Genoese. Despite – or perhaps in compensation for – these losses, the doge Ranieri Zeno mounted a major renovation of the basilica and its surroundings. Where churches typically featured representations of the martyrdom or other scenes from the life of their patron saint, the Venetians placed themselves centre stage in four grand mosaics over the portals of the main facade depicting the ninth-century 'translation' of the body of St Mark from Alexandria to Venice. Today only the fourth and final scene survives, but the first three (which were replaced in the eighteenth century) are vividly represented in Gentile Bellini's 1496 painting *Procession in Piazza San Marco* (illus. 11). Running right to left, they depict two Venetian merchants removing the saint's body from his tomb and loading it onto a boat; the body being loaded on a ship and miraculously saving the ship from a storm on the homeward voyage; and the body being carried in procession through the city of Venice. The fourth image, over the Porta Sant'Alipio, shows the body being carried through the central doorway of San Marco (anachronistically represented in its thirteenth-century form) as a company of distinguished Venetians looks on. Where depictions elsewhere in the basilica show the bishop and other clerics receiving the

12 Porta Sant'Alipio, mosaic, Basilica of San Marco, Venice.

relics, here they have been replaced by a group of patricians, portrayed as a cohesive group, visually belying the bitter rivalries that often divided them (illus. 12).

At the same time, the great space in front of the basilica – today's Piazza San Marco – was paved and made into a stage set for highly choreographed ceremonies designed to represent and perform Venetian piety, splendour and unity. On holy days such as Easter, Pentecost, the feast of St Mark, Christmas and the late January feast in honour of the Virgin, Doge Ranieri Zeno presided over rituals and processions that included participants from the city's many parishes. Most iconic of all was Zeno's transformation of a traditional blessing of the waters into the 'marriage with the sea'. As Martin da Canal described in his *History of Venice*, the doge would exit his palace and cross the Piazza San Marco. At the water's edge:

> he finds his principal ship, boards it with his entire
> entourage and has himself rowed out to sea. And the
> priest who is with Monseignor the doge blesses the

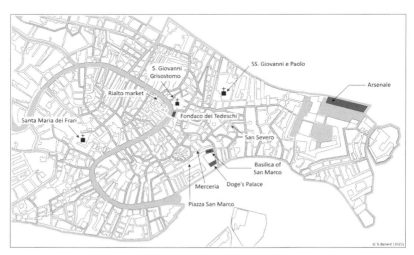

13 Map of Venice.

water and Monseignor the doge throws a golden ring into
the water. And after this Monseignor the doge turns back,
with the same grand solemnity and grand celebration with
which he departed.[6]

For a young Marco witnessing such transformations while his
father and uncle were away in the East, such pageantry would
have formed a standard against which to measure the ceremonies
held at the court of Qubilai Khan.

With all these transformations, the Venice to which the three
Polos returned in 1295 would have looked considerably different
from the one Niccolò and Maffeo had left around 1260. At the
time of their departure, the family had owned property in the
parish of San Severo (in the modern district of Castello). After
their return, they purchased several houses and land in the
parish of San Giovanni Grisostomo (in modern Cannaregio)
on the east side of the Grand Canal, across and slightly upstream
from the Rialto (illus. 13). With the construction of the per-
manent wooden bridge (1264), more and more commerce had
spread across the canal. The Fondaco dei Tedeschi, founded in
1228 to house German merchants from across the Alps, was
nearby in the parish of San Bartolomeo, which also housed
purveyors of spices; mercers and goldsmiths clustered in the
newly paved Merceria and textile merchants in San Giovanni
Grisostomo. Upon returning from Asia, the Polos had relocated
to quarters that were squarely in the heart of Venice's commercial
activity.

Pisa

For today's tourist, Pisa is largely synonymous with its Leaning
Tower, typically visited on a day trip from Florence. In the mid-
twelfth century, however, it struck al-Idrīsī, a Muslim scholar at
the court of the Norman king Roger II of Sicily, as 'one of the

most important and famous cities in Christian lands'. As he
wrote in his geographical compendium, informally known as
the *Book of Roger* (*Kitāb Rujār*):

> Its territory is vast, its markets flourishing, its buildings
> well-populated, its territory extensive, its gardens and
> orchards numerous, its fields adjacent. Its position is
> pre-eminent and its history admirable. Its fortifications
> are high, its lands fertile, its waters abundant, its
> monuments very remarkable. The Pisans have ships
> and horses: that is, they are prepared to launch maritime
> expeditions and attack other localities. This city is on the
> banks of a large river that comes from the mountains of
> Lombardy, on the banks of which are mills and gardens.[7]

For all its favourable geography, Pisa's prosperity – like that
of Venice and Genoa – was built largely through overseas trade.
At the turn of the twelfth century, Pisan merchants benefited

14 Cathedral of Santa Maria Assunta, Pisa.

15 Pisa Griffin on the cathedral of Santa Maria Assunta, Pisa.

from the Crusades to gain trade privileges in the newly founded
crusader states, particularly the county of Antioch. In 1154 a
treaty with the Fatimids granted them commercial foundations
in Alexandria and Cairo in exchange for an agreement not to
take part in any crusader campaigns against Egypt. Pisa's main
sphere of commercial activity, however, was the western
Mediterranean; from the mid-twelfth century it negotiated trade
privileges with Muslim rulers in Tunis (valuable for its strategic
location on the straits connecting the eastern and western
Mediterranean and for its access to North African and sub-
Saharan trade) and in al-Andalus (Islamic Iberia), in sites
including Valencia, Denia and Seville.

   The power and prosperity gained in this overseas trade were
manifest in Pisa's massive cathedral. If the basilica of San Marco
proclaimed Venice's Byzantine ties, Santa Maria Assunta's 'Pisan
Romanesque' style – its grey-and-white marble ground-level
arcades, slender columns and upper galleries – invoked classical
Rome (illus. 14). Construction on the cathedral had begun in
the second half of the eleventh century; in the second half of

16 Pisa Griffin,
Cathedral Museum,
Pisa, c. 1000–1050,
bronze (photograph
c. 1890–1900).

the twelfth, it was augmented by two freestanding structures: a
baptistery (begun in 1153) and campanile – the famous 'Leaning
Tower' (begun in 1173).

Like San Marco but more subtly, Santa Maria Assunta celebrated its city's external triumphs. Two poems inscribed on the
left side of the facade boasted of the booty netted in Pisa's military predations. And perched high atop the east end of Santa
Maria Assunta (illus. 15) was the Pisa Griffin (illus. 16), the largest surviving example of the zoomorphic bronze figures produced
across the eleventh-century Islamic Mediterranean. While considerably less ostentatious than San Marco's bronze hippodrome
horses, it similarly represents the city's claim to Mediterranean
power.

Pisa's intimate connections to North Africa and the Mediterranean appear in one of the most distinctive features of its
architecture: the ceramic plates and bowls (*bacini*) ornamenting
the exterior walls of its eleventh-century churches. Typically

placed in the blind arches just below the roofline, they represent a variety of wares from the city's Islamic trading partners: green and brown ware from Tunisia (by far the most numerous), lustre-ware from Egypt and stamped ware from Spain (illus. 17). Imported for use in Pisan households at a moment when ceramics from the Islamic world were considerably more refined than their Latin European counterparts, as architectural ornaments *bacini* were an economical alternative to the kind of inlaid marble medallions found on the facade of Santa Maria Assunta.

Pisa's Mediterranean connections were also decisive in the life of Leonardo of Pisa or Fibonacci, the most famous mathe-matician of the Latin Middle Ages. Born into the city's merchant elite, he spent his boyhood in Béjaïa (in present-day Algeria) where his father was posted as a 'scribe' (notary and diplomat). With its protected harbour and trade-friendly rulers, Béjaïa was a commercial hub for the export of goods from the local hinter-lands (raw wool, leather, lambskins, alum and wax) as well as from sub-Saharan Africa; and for the import of Flemish, French and Italian wares along with Asian exotica such as spices and

17 *Bacini*, ceramic, Church of San Sisto, Pisa.

balas rubies via transshipment from South and Southeast Asia
through ports like Alexandria. But it was not only the daily minu-
tiae of overseas trade that young Leonardo was called upon to
master; in his own words:

> As my father was a public official away from our homeland
> in the Bugia [Béjaïa] customshouse established for the
> Pisan merchants who frequently gathered there, he had
> me in my youth brought to him, looking to find for me a
> useful and comfortable future; there he wanted me in the
> study of mathematics and to be taught for some days.[8]

So it was that in this bustling North African port, Leonardo
learned the practical algebra pioneered by al-Khwarizmi, the
ninth-century Persian mathematician whose name gives us the
term 'algorithm'. Out of these experiences, he composed his *Book
of Calculation* (*Liber Abaci*), first completed in 1202 and revised
in 1228 for presentation to Emperor Frederick II's court astrol-
oger, the philosopher and polymath Michael Scot. Remembered
today for its pioneering use of algebra and practical mathematics, the *Liber Abaci* clearly reflects merchant interests, focusing
on issues such as currency exchange and conversion, weights
and measures, the loading of ships and price calculations. It
abounds in algebraic word problems built around goods central
to the trade of Béjaïa: '100 *becunias* (goat skins) are worth 42
and ¾ bezants. How much are 21 *becunias* worth?' 'What is the
best way to load a ship, given that a *cantare* of alum weighs as
much as two *cantares* of leather?'[9] Products mentioned include
fustian, Pisan cheese, pepper, saffron, nutmeg, cotton, linen,
grain, oil, sugar and alum. *Mutatis mutandis*, it is easy to imagine
a young Marco Polo, some seven or eight decades after Leonardo,
cutting his teeth over similar problems.

Genoa

Where Venice spanned the myriad islands of its lagoon, Genoa
was crowded against the steep slope of the Ligurian Apennines.
It was only natural for its citizens to take to the sea. Around the
turn of the fourteenth century, when Marco Polo and Rustichello
of Pisa were prisoners in the city, an anonymous Genoese poet
wrote of his compatriots:

> And so many are the Genoese
> And so spread out through the world,
> That wherever one goes and stays
> He makes another Genoa there.[10]

In Marco Polo's day Genoa itself was surrounded by twelfth-
century walls and divided into a patchwork of neighbourhoods
(*alberghi*) dominated by great families like the Doria and the
Grimaldi. Its public buildings could not match the basilica of
San Marco in Venice or the cathedral of Santa Maria Assunta
in Pisa in scale or magnificence. But a new communal palace,
the Palazzo San Giorgio, was commissioned as part of a renewal
of the waterfront in 1260. The cathedral of San Lorenzo, heavily damaged in factional fighting in 1295 (the year of the Polos'
return to Venice) would be rebuilt in the fourteenth century, in
the Gothic style still visible today.

Like its competitors, Genoa had emerged as a Mediterranean
power in the aftermath of the First Crusade; capitalizing on the
commercial privileges it received in the crusader port of Acre, it
established a trade network that included the great emporium
of Alexandria, terminus of the maritime route for the Indian
Ocean trade. At the same time, Genoese merchants were also
expanding into the western Mediterranean, cultivating trade
connections in al-Andalus and North Africa. Competition over

these lucrative commercial routes brought them into conflict with Venetians in the east and Pisans in the west – contests in which the Genoese gained the reputation of being particularly aggressive. Al-Idrīsī, in his *Book of Roger*, described them as 'rich merchants [who] travel by land and by sea who undertake easy and difficult things equally . . . They are experts in ruses of war and in the art of government; among Christians, it is they who have the greatest renown.'[11] Intrepid sailors, the Genoese also ventured past the Pillars of Hercules into the Atlantic, establishing maritime routes to Flanders in 1277 and to England in 1278. Then in 1291 (the year in which the Polos set out for home), two Genoese brothers, Ugolino and Vadino Vivaldi, sailed west into the Atlantic (with two Franciscans on board), trying to reach India – foreshadowing the expeditions of Vasco da Gama and Christopher Columbus two centuries later. They were never heard from again.

Meanwhile, the second half of the thirteenth century brought a series of political and economic realignments. In the late 1250s in the so-called War of Saint Sabas, the Venetians largely ousted the Genoese from the port of Acre, terminus of Asian overland trade routes, thus drastically reducing their presence in the crusader kingdom. But, as we have seen, the Byzantine reconquest of Constantinople in 1261 delivered into Genoese hands the trade privileges previously enjoyed by the Venetians – including, most importantly, access to the Black Sea. To mark this change in fortunes, stones from Constantinople were incorporated as spolia into the Palazzo San Giorgio, then under construction. In the 1270s the Genoese founded a lucrative trading emporium at Caffa (modern Feodosia) in the Crimea, trafficking in regional products such as grain, wax, furs and salted fish but also in slaves, destined for both Mamluk Egypt and Latin Europe. At the same time, once the Mongols established their rule over Persia, the Genoese assiduously cultivated political and diplomatic relations with the Ilkhans (descendants of Qubilai's brother Hülegü). In the 1280s they were prominent among the Italians who flocked to the Ilkhanid capital of Tabriz (in present-day northwestern Iran). In 1289 a Genoese merchant named Buscarello de' Ghizolfi carried letters from the Ilkhan Arghun to kings Philip IV of France and Edward I of England, proposing an alliance (never realized) against the Mamluks of Egypt – one of several times he served as an official envoy to the West. By 1290 several hundred Genoese were building ships for Arghun in Mesopotamia, and in the *Description*, Marco Polo notes Genoese merchants sailing the Caspian Sea (§23).

In his *Chronicle of the City of Genoa* (*Chronicon januense*), Archbishop Jacopo da Varagine proclaimed 'now' to be 'the time of [the city's] perfection', dating this pre-eminence from 1133, when it had been elevated to an archbishopric. Since that time, 'it increased greatly in riches and glory' to the point that 'its magnificence has challenged the power of kings, the Saracen people, the city of the Venetians, and even the city of the Pisans.'[12] Indeed, the second half of the thirteenth century was punctuated by triumphs. In 1284 hostilities with Pisa, spurred by competition over the islands of Corsica and Elba, culminated in a massive naval victory in the Battle of Meloria, off the Tuscan coast. As Jacopo da Varagine later described this 'great triumph': 'From that time onward the Genoese so humiliated and over-powered the Pisans that up to the present day [1296] they have kept their galleys in port and prohibited other vessels from entering there.'[13] In 1290 the Genoese destroyed Pisa's port, carrying off the harbour chains that had previously protected it from enemy ships, hanging pieces of them as trophies around Genoa: on the city gates, on the facade of the Palazzo San Giorgio and on various neighbourhood churches – including San Matteo, the family church of Oberto Doria, the victorious admiral at Meloria (illus. 18).

18 Church of San Matteo, Genoa.

In 1287 a Nestorian Christian monk named Rabban Sauma, an envoy from the Ilkhan Arghun, passed through Genoa bearing messages to the pope and the kings of France and England. He was enthusiastically welcomed by 'a great crowd of people' who escorted him to the cathedral of San Lorenzo and made a point of showing him its relics. These included a silver coffer containing the ashes of John the Baptist, the city's patron, looted in 1099 from Myra (on the southern coast of Anatolia) by Genoese ships returning from the First Crusade; and a six-sided translucent green bowl, which, Rabban Sauma is told, was the emerald paten 'from which our Lord ate the Passover with His disciples . . . brought there when Jerusalem was captured' (in 1099).[14] Interestingly, the archbishop Jacopo da Varagine remained aggressively agnostic on the provenance of the object, still housed in the Treasury Museum of the Cathedral of San Lorenzo today and known as the Holy Basin (*Sacro Catino*) (illus. 19):

We do not know whether this is true – because nothing
is impossible with God, we neither assert it absolutely nor
deny it obstinately. Thus anyone who wishes to believe
it must not be argued with out of fun, and anyone who
does not wish to believe it must not be reproved out of
rashness.

For Jacopo, the vessel – today identified as glass, probably of
Islamic origin – stands, rather, as proof of the superiority of

19 *Sacro Catino*, 1st century CE, glass, Treasury Museum of the
Cathedral of San Lorenzo, Genoa.

20 Nymphaion, embroidered silk of St Lawrence, 1261.

divine power over human artifice, 'because things made in this
way are fully perfect to the point that neither nature nor human
artifice can add anything to their perfection'.[15]

We do not know the precise circumstances under which
Marco Polo and Rustichello of Pisa were brought to Genoa as
captives, but we may be sure the welcome they received was
quite different from that accorded Rabban Sauma. They may
likely have been shown trophies of Genoese triumphs over their
hometowns – especially the pieces of Pisa's harbour chain fes-
tooning the city gates and the Palazzo San Giorgio. In 1291 the
latter, originally built as the seat of the communal government,
had been converted into Genoa's customs house – perhaps the
place where Marco and Rustichello were imprisoned. If they
were shown the cathedral, they would have seen (alongside the
ashes of St John the Baptist and the *Sacro Catino*) the magnificent embroidered silk commemorating the Genoese–Byzantine
alliance sealed by the 1261 Treaty of Nymphaion – part of the
political realignment that had resulted in the Venetians' expul-
sion from Constantinople and control of the lucrative Black
Sea trade. Especially poignant for both Marco and Rustichello
would have been three scenes (out of the twenty illustrating St
Lawrence's life and martyrdom) depicting the saint's imprison-
ment (illus. 20). The misfortunes of war had brought both men
to Genoa at the culmination of the three decades marking the

height of Genoese prosperity, leading even Archbishop Jacopo of Varagine (who would die in the same year that they penned their *Description*) to boast that Genoa 'is of the greatest service to Italians because its citizens transport goods from lands beyond the sea which they share with other cities'.[16]

In September 1298, when Marco and Rustichello were likely already captive in Genoa, a great naval battle was fought off Curzola on the Dalmatian coast. As an anonymous continuation to the archbishop's *Chronicle of the City of Genoa* records, 7,000 Venetians perished; of the 8,000 who were captured, most were taken to Genoa. The following year, the Genoese, 'moved by the . . . urging of the [ruler] of Milan as well as by mercy, and wishing to recognize God for such a blessing', made peace with Venice and freed all its Venetian captives; there soon followed a peace with Pisa, and Genoa subsequently released its Pisan prisoners as well – presumably allowing both Marco and Rustichello to return to their homes.[17]

An Interconnected World

The future St Francis (illus. 21), who died in Assisi in 1226, and the great Mongol conqueror Chinggis Khan (illus. 22), who died on campaign in 1227, inhabited separate worlds. However, that was about to change suddenly as successive waves of Mongol conquests produced what is conventionally described as the largest contiguous land empire the world has ever seen. In 1237 the third generation of Chinggis Khan's successors launched a campaign into Eastern Europe, taking Kyiv in 1240 and sweeping westward into Poland and Hungary – an invasion so unprecedented and cataclysmic that, as the English chronicler Matthew Paris famously recorded, fleets from Gothland and Friesland failed to make their regular journeys to Yarmouth, adversely affecting the price of herring on the east coast of England.

21 Giotto, *St Francis of Assisi Receiving the Stigmata*, c. 1300–1325, tempera and gold on wood.

22 Anonymous, *Chinggis Khan*, 1294, album leaf, ink and colours on silk.

Within two decades of St Francis's death, however, one of his followers, John of Plano Carpini, travelling in 1245–7 at the behest of Pope Innocent IV, reached the Mongol capital just in time to witness the acclamation of Chinggis's grandson Güyük as Great Khan; a few years later (1253–5) another Franciscan, William of Rubruck, journeyed to the court of Güyük's successor, Möngke (r. 1251–9), on behalf of the French king Louis IX (r. 1226–70). Both wrote long reports, in Latin, for their respective sponsors, chronicling their experiences and including extensive descriptions of the Mongols. By the time Marco was born in 1254, the worlds of Latin Europe and Mongol Asia had thus come together.

The decade following Marco's birth brought even more momentous political changes. In 1258 the Mongols conquered Baghdad and executed the last Abbasid caliph, ending the line that had presided over Sunni Islam for more than five hundred years. Qubilai's younger brother Hülegü took power as 'Ilkhan' – that is, ruler subordinate to the khagan: first his eldest brother Möngke, then to the latter's successor Qubilai. The 1250s also brought political turmoil to Muslim-ruled lands of the eastern Mediterranean. The Ayyubids, descendants of the fabled twelfth-century leader Saladin (Salah al-Din), having weathered a crusade led by Louis ix in 1248–54, were displaced by the Mamluks – slave-soldiers who would rule Egypt and Syria until the Ottoman conquest of 1517. This reordering of the political chessboard mattered hugely to the merchants of Venice, Genoa and other Latin Christian trading powers, threatening their access to the Mediterranean port city of Alexandria, the western terminus of one of two great maritime routes to India and entrepôt for the spices and other precious commodities from the east. Then in 1260 the Mamluk sultan Baybars defeated a Mongol army at the Battle of Ayn Jalut, marking the western limit of Mongol expansion in the Middle East.

In the meantime, the territory conquered by the Mongols, nominally under the rule of a single Great Khan since the time of Chinggis, had effectively split into four major realms (illus. 23). The vast regions to the northwest conquered in the campaigns of the late 1230s and ruled by descendants of Chinggis Khan's eldest son Jochi are today known as the khanate of the Golden Horde (Marco Polo's 'Tartars of the West'); it is these lands – including the vast steppes of modern Ukraine north of the Black Sea and extending into Eastern Europe north of the Danube

– that had enticed the elder Polos on their first journey east from Constantinople in 1260 (§§2–3). Hülegü's conquest of the Abbasid caliphate resulted in the establishment of the Ilkhanate (Marco's 'Tartars of the East'), controlling the heartland of Persia from its capital at Tabriz and with influence reaching west into Anatolia. The Ilkhans frequently clashed with their Jochid cousins over the valuable grazing lands and trade routes on the border between their two khanates (§§222–7); it was one such conflict, blocking the elder Polos' return to Constantinople, that had led them to travel further east in the first place, eventually landing in the Silk Road city of Bukhara (§§3–4). Throughout the Polos' time in Asia, the Ilkhans remained Qubilai's most dependable allies. Despite the distance separating them, the two courts stayed in close contact, exchanging advisors and technical experts in ways that advanced scientific knowledge and inflected artistic and artisanal production in both realms. The heartland of Central Asia was ruled by descendants of Chinggis Khan's second son Chaghadai, perennially at odds with Qubilai and the Ilkhans (both descended from Chinggis's youngest son,

23 Map of Central Asia showing significant sites in Marco Polo's world.

Tolui). Controlling the rugged lands associated with the ancient Silk Road, the Chaghadids were the Mongols who most closely retained traditional nomadic ways – in contrast to their Toluid cousins who progressively adapted to the cultures of the great sedentary empires under their rule. The endemic conflict among these khanates disrupted land routes through Central Asia. This is one reason why Qubilai's embassy to the Ilkhanate in the early 1290s – giving the Polos the opportunity to return to Venice – took the maritime route across the Indian Ocean and through the Persian Gulf (§19).

The most important and powerful of the Mongol khanates, however, was indisputably that of Qubilai, who had succeeded his elder brother Möngke as khagan in 1260. Today, we often take Marco Polo's time in the East as synonymous with his discovery of 'China'. In the *Description*, however, he divides the lands of the Great Khan into Cathay, the lands the Mongols had conquered from the Jin dynasty in 1234, and 'Mangi', the Southern Song Empire, definitively captured only in 1279, after the Polos' arrival. This conquest reconstituted a Chinese empire that had not existed as such for several centuries. In keeping with Chinese tradition, Qubilai adopted a name, Yuan, for his ruling line, founding a dynasty that would last until 1368, when it was displaced by the Ming, who went on to rule China until 1644.

As they expanded their empire by conquest, Chinggis and his immediate successors Ögödei (1229–41), Güyük (1246–50) and Möngke (1251–9) restructured their rule, the better to exploit the resources and productivity of their new subject lands and peoples. At the same time, they struggled to strike an equilibrium between their own centralizing power and the centrifugal forces of subordinate khans and regional governors. These innovations included Ögödei's creation of 'Branch Secretariats' (1229) to oversee civilian (as opposed to military) organization. Most relevant for understanding the role Marco Polo may have played during his time in Qubilai's service was the four-part division of Chinese society: the top tier held by the Mongols, the third consisting of northern Chinese of the former Jin dynasty and the fourth of the Chinese of the Southern Song Empire, conquered in 1279. The second tier, called *semu ren* (varied peoples), was comprised largely of Central and West Asians – Turks, Persians and Arabs – charged with many of the administrative functions of empire. It is surely amid this multilingual corps of bureaucrats, technocrats and diplomats that Marco and the elder Polos would have found their place during their two-and-a-half decades in Asia.

A Multilingual World

In the prologue to the *Description*, Rustichello of Pisa reports that when the young Marco Polo, then aged about twenty, first arrived at the Mongol court, 'he learned to read and write four languages.' One of them, naturally enough, was Mongolian: 'he learned the Tartars' customs, languages, and writing so well that it was a marvel' (§16, p. 10). Now Marco, of course, would have left home speaking his native Venetian, and presumably with at least an elementary knowledge of Latin and perhaps also French. That he should first have learned Mongolian is natural enough; the elder Polos, on their own first visit to Qubilai Khan, had been able to respond to all the questions put to them about 'my lord the pope . . . the Roman church, and all the customs of the Latins . . . like the wise men that they were' since they were 'well acquainted with the language of the Tartars' (§7, p. 5). What Marco's other three languages may have been we are never explicitly told.

Spanning a vast territory populated by diverse peoples both sedentary and nomadic, the Mongol Empire was multilingual by necessity and design. While Mongol served as its 'official' language, the khans – in common with other premodern rulers – were never interested in imposing their language or culture on their conquered subjects; instead, they employed interpreters and translators drawn from an army of bureaucrats composed of local intelligentsia, merchants and other polyglot adventurers. In Ilkhanid Persia the court historian Rashid al-Din credited Qubilai's great grand-nephew Ghazan, who assumed power in the same year that the Polos finally returned home to Venice, with a knowledge of 'Arabic, Persian, Hindi, Kashmiri, Tibetan, Chinese, Frankish, and a smattering of other languages' along with his native Mongolian.[18] Even allowing for a generous dose of flattery on the part of Rashid al-Din, this list captures how much multilingualism was prized across the medieval world, and why Marco's facility with languages would have helped attract Qubilai's attention and favour.

One remarkable manuscript documenting the linguistic complexity of this world is the so-called *Codex Cumanicus*. Likely compiled by Genoese merchants in the Crimean peninsula in the 1290s (as the Polos were returning to Venice and Marco was composing his *Description*), it contains a trilingual glossary in a vulgar Latin inflected with Italianate features; a simplified Persian, which served as a lingua franca for merchants across Asia; and a rather ungrammatical form of Cuman, the Turkic language of the nomadic peoples who had dominated the steppes of present-day Ukraine before the Mongol expansion of the 1230s and '40s. It opens with a grammatical section (lists of conjugated verbs, adverbs, nouns and pronouns), followed by words sorted into rough categories: spiritual matters (God, angel, peace, charity, paradise, hell), the four elements (air, water, earth, fire), the four humours, expressions of time (year, month, day, night, the canonical hours, days of the week and months of the year), the five senses, terms related to weather and the directions, qualities like goodness, beauty, length and health, a long list of spices,

items related to various trades, colours, precious stones, body
parts, kinship terms, things pertaining to war, the home, horses;
and concluding with trees, animals, birds and miscellaneous
foodstuffs.[19]

Describing the World

This brings us back to the fortuitous collaboration between Marco
Polo of Venice and Rustichello of Pisa in 1298. One surprising
result of Genoa's victories over Pisa at Meloria and in other
battles was the use they made of their prisoners of war. Since
many of their captives were notaries, they were put to work
making copies of texts in Latin, French and Italian. Among the
most popular French texts were histories of the ancient world
(like the *Histoire ancienne jusqu'à César*) and Arthurian romances
– including the earliest version of Rustichello's own compilation
of Arthurian material from the Tristan tradition. Several manuscripts produced in this coerced scriptorium conclude with
telling explicits (endnotes by the author or scribe) in which the
copyist records his name and identifies himself as Pisan and a
captive in Genoa. A French translation of three Latin moral
treatises contains a poignant appeal in French verse for the
reader to pray to God to extract him from prison and grant him
freedom in this life and 'the glory of Paradise' in the hereafter.[20]
Imagining imprisoned Pisans passing their captivity labouring
over manuscripts – many in French – gives a vivid backdrop
to the circumstances leading to the composition of Marco's
Description of the World.

24 Anige, *Qubilai Khan*, 1294, album leaf, ink and colours on silk.

TWO

The Book of the Great Khan

Now I want to start telling you in this book about all the very great deeds and all the very great marvels of the Great Khan now reigning, who is called Qubilai Khan; in our language, this means great lord of lords. And certainly he is rightly called this, for everyone knows in truth that this Great Khan is the most powerful in men, land, and treasure that the world has ever seen or who ever will be, from Adam our first father until now.
Description §76, p. 67

The second title by which the *Description of the World* was known in the Middle Ages was *The Book of the Great Khan* (*Li livres du Grant Caam*). The French manuscripts bearing this title all date from after Marco Polo's death but are among the best-known surviving medieval versions because of their beautiful, lavishly executed illuminations. The copy today housed in the British Library in London (Royal MS 19 D I) was made around 1336 for the French king Philip VI as he prepared for a crusade that never materialized; in this anthology, Marco Polo's text is preceded by two accounts of Alexander the Great and followed by a miscellany that includes two travel accounts, a crusade treatise, excerpts from a French historical chronicle and a French translation of the Bible (illus. 25). The second, MS Bodl. 264 of the Bodleian Library in Oxford, made around the first decade of the fifteenth century, contains a text that closely

follows that of the Royal MS 19 D I, again combined with two
versions of the Alexander legend (one in Old French and one
in Middle English); its illustrations, though placed identically
to those in the Royal MS 19 D I, compositionally and stylistically
parallel those in the Old French *Alexander* romance, thus bringing the two texts into close visual as well as thematic alignment
(illus. 26).

To return to our text: the epigraph above follows a series of
chapters that narrate the rise of the Mongols under Chinggis
Khan and his successors and give ethnographic descriptions

25 Miniature from Marco Polo, *Li livres du Grant Caam*,
1333– c. 1340, depicting Niccolò and Maffeo Polo with Emperor
Baldwin of Constantinople; the Polo brothers before the Patriarch;
and the Polo brothers sailing for the Black Sea.

26 The Great Khan's feast, miniature from Marco Polo, *Li livres du Grant Caam*, 1338–1410.

(resembling accounts penned by Franciscans John of Plano Carpini and William of Rubruck) of their life on the steppes. It inaugurates what is arguably the heart of the book: the history of Qubilai Khan's rise to power and a description of his capital at Khanbaliq (modern Beijing) and its great festivals; it then traces the path of his itinerant court and concludes with some of the features of his empire calculated to elicit the wonder of his Western European readers (§§76–104). The passage itself is extraordinary. In medieval French epic and romance, the tradition to which Rustichello of Pisa belongs, heroes are exalted by being favourably compared to Alexander the Great, Julius Caesar, Charlemagne, Arthur or other famous figures of history or legend. Here, on the other hand, Qubilai Khan is alone on his stage, eluding any comparison in the history of mankind. This is all the more remarkable since Qubilai, the man, is far from imposing: 'he is of good size, neither small nor big, but of medium height. He is pleasingly fleshy; all his members are very well shaped. His face is white and red as a rose; his eyes black and beautiful; his nose well made and just right' (§82, p. 72). A pleasant and middling figure, he is nevertheless the greatest ruler the world has ever seen, fully justifying the *Description*'s second title, *The Book of the Great Khan*.

Though Qubilai had died in 1294, the year before the Polos arrived back in Venice, word was slow to reach the West and in 1298, Marco and Rustichello still wrote of the Great Khan as if he were alive. Meanwhile, the Chinese painter, poet and polymath Zhao Mengfu commemorated the great ruler in a verse entitled 'A Eulogy of the Sagely Virtue of His Imperial Majesty':

> Emperor Shih-tsu (Qubilai Khan)
> East the ocean, west the Himalaya,
> dwelling for great monarchs!
> Southern barges, northern horses
> throng the royal capital.
> The great man of this period
> descended from heaven above;
> over ten thousand miles – standard axles and script:
> no precedent in the past.
> Ch'in and Han were powerful,
> but tyrannical and cruel;
> Chin and T'ang were beautiful,
> but lacked a noble scheme.
> Weaving heaven and earth together,
> far-reaching in its rules;
> generations of god-like grandsons
> will venerate your Sagely Plan.[1]

In a few short lines Zhao Mengfu vividly conjures the geographical reach of the Great Khan's power – from the Himalayas to
the Pacific and (paralleling Marco's claim that he is the greatest ruler since 'Adam our first father' (§76, p. 67)) says he had
'no precedent in the past'. Perhaps tellingly, however, while he
explicitly names 'Ch'in and Han', 'Chin and T'ang', this scion
of the imperial house only recently conquered by the Mongols
pointedly omits the Southern Song from his litany of previous
dynasties falling short of Qubilai's grandeur.

What makes him so exceptional? Marco and Rustichello, as
we have seen, emphasize 'all the very great deeds and all the
very great marvels of the Great Khan now reigning' (*Description*
§76, p. 67). His deeds are told in accounts of his victories over
various Mongol rivals and in his conquest of the Southern Song.
What about the marvels? Now, the fascination with marvels was
widespread across the medieval world. Loosely combining what
exceeded the everyday, tales of the marvellous proliferated across
genres such as natural philosophy, travel literature, romance and,
especially, the miracles of saints and holy figures. Meanwhile, if
the third title given to Marco's text in the late Middle Ages was
The Book of Marvels (*Le Livre des merveilles*), this was arguably
less because of the natural and supernatural wonders sprinkled
throughout the work, but rather the distinctive and – for Western
European readers – exotic aspects of the Mongol Empire and its
administration, assembled in the figure of Qubilai Khan.

The Marvels of Empire

When the Mongols made their first incursion into Eastern Europe
in 1237, the terror they sowed spread the length of the Latin West.
Citing reports relayed to the English king Henry III, the chronicler Matthew Paris, writing in the abbey of St Albans, northwest
of London, described them as a 'monstrous and inhuman race

of men' that had 'burst forth from the northern mountains', speaking an unknown language, feeding on raw flesh 'and even on human beings'.[2] From the outset, then, the Mongols – unknown from Latin Christendom's traditional sources of knowledge in scripture and classical authors – were associated with chaos, violence and disorder. Soon, however, the eyewitness accounts that began filtering back to Western rulers gave multiple examples of the strict order of Mongol society. In the 1240s John of Plano Carpini detailed the decimal organization of their armies, common to Central Asian nomads: 'over ten men [is] set one man and he is what we call a captain of ten; over ten of these [is] placed one, named a captain of a hundred,' and so on up to ten thousand.[3] In the 1250s William of Rubruck described the tent-city of the khan of the Golden Horde:

> When they unload the dwellings, the chief wife pitches
> her residence at the westernmost end, and the others
> follow according to rank, so that the last wife will be
> at the eastern end: there is the space of a stone's throw
> between the residence of one lady and the next.[4]

In less than two decades Matthew Paris's 'monstrous and inhuman race of men' were transformed into a well-ordered society.

In this context it is striking how many of the wonders that Marco Polo ascribes to the Mongols have to do with their penchant for organization and their stewardship of empire. One of the most extraordinary phenomena that he encountered was the *yam*: the famed postal relay that made it possible for the Mongols to transmit messages across the breadth of their vast empire with lightning speed. Such postal relays had a long history in Asia, dating back to the Achaemenid Empire in Persia and the Han dynasty in China. But given the extent of their conquests, the Mongols' network functioned on an unprecedented scale. In

The Secret History of the Mongols, an oral-based narrative compiled around the middle of the thirteenth century, the Great Khan Ögödei specifies that 'set[ting] up post-stations so that my envoys would swiftly ride between us post-haste and also transport needs and necessities' was the second of four deeds that he had added to the accomplishments of his father, Chinggis Khan.[5] Under Qubilai, the *yam* came under the supervision of the Bureau for Transmission Services, with offices in the capitals of Dadu and Shangdu; among other things, the Bureau oversaw postal relay inspectors whose remit was to seek out or investigate abuses of the network. According to the *Yuan Shi* (the official history of the Yuan dynasty, compiled, in traditional fashion, in the early years of the Ming), by the end of Qubilai's reign the *yam* comprised over 1,400 stations, 50,000 horses, 1,400 oxen, 6,700 mules, 4,000 carts, 6,000 boats, 200 dogs and 1,150 sheep.

Marco adds colour and detail to this bureaucratic tally. Post stations, he writes, are found on 'all the main roads going to the provinces', at intervals of 40 or 50 kilometres (25–30 mi.) or 55–65 kilometres (35–40 mi.) in more 'out-of-the-way places'. Each is stocked with 'between 300 and 400 horses' levied from the surrounding country; here, messengers find 'a very large and beautiful palace' featuring 'a very rich bed, adorned with fine silk sheets' where even a king would be well-lodged. Then, Marco adds 'something that I had forgotten': a network of runners, posted at 3-mile intervals, who go full out between stages, wearing belts adorned with bells to alert the relay runners at the following station. 'I tell you that in this way . . . the great lord gets news from ten days' journey away in a day and a night . . . I tell you that such men as these often bring the lord fruit from ten days away in one day' (§98, pp. 89–90).

Despite the length and specificity of Marco's account, we should not take all of his details at face value. Particularly in more remote parts of the empire, local conditions (including rebellions or hostilities between rival Mongol factions) could disrupt existing routes – as when troubles with his cousin Qaidu, who 'was never at peace with the Great Khan, but always at war' (§199, p. 193), prompted Qubilai to establish an alternate route to Ilkhanid Persia (his lone ally among the other Mongol khanates) along the southern rim of the Tarim Basin. As historian Thomas Allsen has noted, fixed routes and permanently staffed relay stations of the kind Marco describes 'prevailed around major political centers, in some densely populated regions, and at threatened frontiers'.[6] This is probably also the way we should read Marco's glowing description of imperial highways and byways:

> Now know in all truth that the great lord has ordered trees planted along the major roads traveled by messengers, merchants, and other people – two paces apart; and I tell you that they are large enough to be seen from afar. The Great Khan had this done so that everyone could see the road and not get lost: for you will find these trees on out-of-the-way roads – a great comfort to merchants and sellers. This goes for all provinces and all kingdoms. (§100, p. 91)

Elsewhere 'in the heart of the continent and the steppe', no such fixed infrastructure existed; arrangements were much more flexible and ad hoc, so that the postal network, so often taken as a hallmark of the Mongol Empire, is better seen as 'part of the nomads' standard logistical repertoire even in periods marked by political disintegration'.[7] Nevertheless, for Marco this network of riders, horses and resources remains 'such a marvelous thing, of such great worth that it can hardly be described or written' (§98, p. 89).

Another of the wonders of Qubilai's empire, to which Marco devotes an entire chapter, is 'How the Great Khan distributes

notes for money'. He begins rather enigmatically: 'It is true that
the great lord's mint is located in this city of Khanbaliq. It is
established in such a way that you could well say that the Great
Khan knows its secrets perfectly; and I will show you how' (§96,
p. 86). The word he uses for 'mint' is *secque* – an Old French rendering of the Venetian *zecca* (itself derived from the Arabic
sikka) for the die used to stamp coins. But the 'secrets' Marco goes
on to describe could not be farther from Venetian coinage:

> Now know that he has money made in the way I will tell
> you: he takes tree bark – from mulberry trees, whose fronds
> are eaten by the worms who make silk – and the inner bark
> between the bark and wood of the tree; and from this inner
> bark, he has notes made like paper; these are all black.
> When these notes are made, he has them cut so as to make
> a small one worth half of a little *tornesello*; another, still
> small, is worth one *tornesello*; another is worth half a
> Venetian silver groat; another is worth 2 groats; another
> 5 groats, another 10 groats; another one bezant; and
> another 3, and so on up to 10 bezants. (§96, pp. 86–7)

Elsewhere, Marco twice mentions mulberry trees in connection
with silk production (§§107, 111, pp. 94, 97); by the turn of
the fourteenth century, many in the West would have known
that silkworms feed on mulberry leaves, so although this is his
first mention of the tree, he rushes past that fact to focus on the
incomparably greater marvel of paper money. Even this brief
introduction was likely to tantalize a contemporary audience.
First, by the end of the thirteenth century paper was being produced in Italy (the town of Fabriano in the Marche of Ancona
pioneered the use of watermarks in 1282) but it was manufactured not from tree bark but from rags. More importantly, the
currencies used throughout Europe and the Islamic world were

of course metal coinage: in Marco Polo's day, *tornesello* was the Venetian name for the *denier tournois*, a 20 per cent silver coin used in the Frankish principalities in mainland Greece; Venice would begin minting its own *tornesello* in 1353. The *grosso*, or groat, was a large silver coin minted from the late twelfth century (illus. 27), while *bezant* was the name for the Byzantine hyperpyron, a gold coin that circulated throughout the Balkans and served as the money of account in Frankish Greece. Venice had begun minting its own gold ducats in 1284 during Marco's absence, though here he continues to cite the older currency as his standard of reference.

Paper money was not a Mongol innovation: it had been used under the preceding dynasties – the Tang, the Song and the Jin (the latter in response to a shortage of copper for coinage). Qubilai's predecessor and elder brother Möngke had created a Superintendency of Paper Money in 1253. But Qubilai, who established a Ministry of Revenue (one of six new ministries he founded), took the use of paper money to unprecedented levels, and the terms on which bills were issued and the infrastructure of governmental agencies regulating them were recalibrated more than once during his reign (illus. 28). Bills bore inscriptions in Chinese, accompanied by a partial transliteration into Phagspa (the new script Qubilai had specially commissioned to record all the languages of his empire, and which was named

27 Venetian silver *grosso* minted under Doge Lorenzo Tiepolo (1268–75).

28 Paper money
of the Yuan
dynasty.

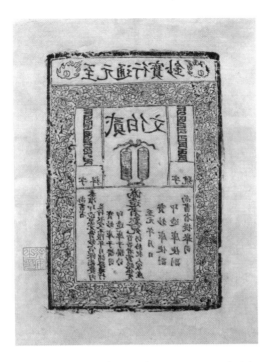

after its creator, the Tibetan lama Phagspa) – an unmistakable visual sign of Mongol authority. Beyond paper money's ideological and economic functions, Marco underscores its physical properties: 'I also tell you', he says, 'that the note that is used for 10 bezants weighs less than one.' The benefits of such easily portable currency are obvious – particularly in China, where heavy 'strings' of coins with square holes punched in their centre had sometimes served as units of currency. Since paper was much less durable, however, notes that had been in circulation got torn and damaged; then 'you take them to the mint where they are exchanged for new and fresh ones,' losing only 3 per cent of the value of bills being redeemed.

Even more remarkable is the way these bills are deployed to exert control on the flow of commodities and merchandise throughout Qubilai's empire:

When these notes are made in the way I have described
to you, he pays for everything with them and has them
distributed through all the provinces, kingdoms, and lands
under his rule; and no one dares refuse them, on pain
of losing his life. I also tell you that all the people and
populated regions under his rule willingly take these notes
in payment, because with them they'll go and make all
their payments [for] merchandise, pearls, precious stones,
gold, and silver. You can buy everything with them; and
they make payments with the notes I have described.
(§96, p. 87)

As throughout the *Description*, Rustichello's repetition of phrases
like 'I also tell you' serve as the italic emphasis and exclamation
points demanding our attention or asserting the truth of features
most likely to arouse the scepticism of his medieval audience.
In this passage two things strain credulity: first, that this currency
is valid 'through all the provinces, kingdoms, and lands' under
Qubilai's rule, in contrast to the proliferation of currencies circu-
lating in Western Europe; and second, that, under pain of death,
these pieces of paper may be exchanged for 'merchandise, pearls,
precious stones, *gold, and silver*' (emphasis added).

The circulation of paper money, it turns out, is but one ele-
ment of a system that ensured the centripetal flow of goods to
the heart of Qubilai's empire. Several times a year, Marco continues, merchants are required by decree to bring 'pearls, precious
stones, gold, silver, and other things (that is, cloth of gold and
silk)' to be appraised by 'twelve wise men', experts appointed by
the Great Khan, in exchange for paper notes. The value of these
goods amounts to 'a good four hundred thousand bezants' each
year. Merchants, for their part, take the paper money 'most willingly, and use it for all the things they buy throughout the lands
of the great lord' while Qubilai, in turn, gets all the gold, silver,

pearls and precious stones from all his lands. Nevertheless, Marco quickly defuses any anxiety or discontent that might arise from this indication of the Great Khan's monopoly: 'if a man wishes to buy gold or silver to make his tableware or his belt or his other objects, he goes to the great lord's mint bringing these notes, and he gives them as payment for the gold and silver he buys from the lord of the mint' (§96, p. 87).

As we have seen, the Mongols are better known for the terror they sowed and the devastation they wrought during their campaigns of conquest than for their orderly rule. In his description of the 'large and noble city' of Balkh (in modern-day Afghanistan), Marco notes that 'in former times it was a good deal nobler and larger, for the Tartars and other people laid it waste and ravaged it' – its many beautiful palaces and marble houses 'are still there, [but] ruined and wasted' (§45, p. 36). The Old French words he uses for 'laid waste' and 'wasted' – *gastés, gastee* – evoke the *terre gaste* of the twelfth- and thirteenth-century versions of the story of Perceval and the Grail (the tradition culminating in T. S. Eliot's celebrated 1922 poem 'The Waste Land'). So we do not necessarily expect to find, in Marco's account of Qubilai's rule, a chapter entitled 'How the Great Khan helps his people in need of grain and animals'. It begins:

> Now also know in truth that the great lord sends his
> messengers throughout his lands and kingdoms and
> provinces to find out from his men if they have had
> damage to their grain, whether from bad weather,
> locusts, or other plagues. If he finds that any peoples
> have sustained damages and have no grain, he does not
> take from them the tribute that they owe him that year
> but has them given some of his crops so that they have
> something to sow and eat; and this is really a great good
> done by the lord. (§99, p. 91)

We can measure the significance Marco accords to this phenomenon from the way he returns to it in a subsequent chapter, filling in the details and logistics of this system for grain distribution:

> Now know that it is true that when the great lord sees
> that grain is in great abundance and that it is inexpensive,
> he amasses a very great quantity and has it put in a house
> and has it so well watched that it does not spoil for three
> years or four. Understand that he stockpiles all grains
> – wheat, barley, millet, rice, panic, and other grains –
> and has a very great amount of these grains assembled.
> (§103, p. 92)

Once again, Rustichello's emphatic 'Now know . . .' and 'Understand' show us how extraordinary this is. Dadu's granaries are strategically located: one between the southeast corner of the Imperial City and the outer wall (near the Central Secretariat), others along the capital's eastern wall, between the Chongren and Chihui Gate. In amassing this surplus in times of plenty, the Great Khan shows great generosity: 'if a measure is selling for a bezant, I mean of wheat, he gives four for it'; his benevolence reaches far and wide: 'thus everyone has his fill and abundance of grain . . . and he does this for all the lands under his authority' (§103, p. 92). While these measures are designed to benefit all those across his empire, Qubilai shows special concern for the people of Khanbaliq:

> for everyone who goes to court to get some of the lord's
> bread, none is denied . . . every day more than 3,000 go
> . . . This is quite a great goodness, that the lord takes pity
> on his poor people, and the people hold him in such great
> regard that they pray to him like a god. (§104, p. 92)

Qubilai's attention to agricultural resources and production exemplifies how flexibly he adapted to the needs of his people. In the early stages of the Mongols' transition from steppe warriors to rulers of a great sedentary empire, agriculture was not such a priority. According to the *Yuan Shi*, the original plans for Dadu had designated the areas outside the city walls as grassland for grazing the myriad horses the Mongols required for their cavalry and postal service. But Chabi, Qubilai's chief wife (d. 1281), stepped in to assure that the allotments already made to local farmers, on whose crops the Chinese population depended, were respected. Qubilai's change of heart, and his redistribution system, could not have been better timed. His reign coincided with the first stages of an extended period of colder weather and climatic instability that would last into the nineteenth century. This climate change provoked floods that began in the 1280s, becoming widespread in 1295, then recurring almost annually in the new century; famines occurred every other year between 1268 and 1272. The Great Khan's largesse would have struck a chord with Marco and Rustichello's readers: from about 1270, agricultural production also fell in the West, leading to a series of serious famines by the beginning of the fourteenth century.

Amid this careful stewardship of his empire's agricultural resources, Qubilai did not forget the needs of his pastoralist subjects. Describing the logistics of collecting and redistributing surpluses of grain, Marco specifies:

> He does this in summer. In the winter, he does the same for those who live off their animals. For if there are found to be men whose animals have died from diseases that have come to them, he gives them some of his animals and helps them and does not take tribute that year. In this way, as I have told you, the great lord helps and sustains his men. (§99, p. 91)

Taken together, Marco's first-hand account of the provisions made to ensure the welfare of both his Chinese-agriculturalist and his nomadic-pastoralist subjects neatly captures the flexibility and adaptability of Mongol rule.

A Tale of Three Cities

Chapter One began with portraits of Venice, Pisa and Genoa, adding detail and colour to our portrait of thirteenth-century Europe. Moving to the other side of the world, we turn the spotlight on three of the great metropolises of Yuan China: Qubilai's capital of Khanbaliq (modern Beijing), the former Southern Song capital of Quinsai (modern Hangzhou) and Zaytun (modern Quanzhou), the great port on the South China Sea. Outsized on a scale unimaginable in the West, they in many ways outstrip the more conventional marvels found in the *Description* – contributing, rather, to the greatness of the Great Khan.

Khanbaliq

When the Polos first arrived in Khanbaliq (Chinese Dadu) in the mid-1270s, it was a city under construction. The Mongols' previous capital, Qaraqorum, was located on the Central Asian steppe south of Lake Baikal, with Shang-tu ('Upper Capital') – Samuel Taylor Coleridge's fabled 'Xanadu' – some 350 kilometres (217 mi.) northwest of Dadu, as their summer capital. In 1266 Qubilai ordered a new winter capital built on a site adjacent to the ruins of Zhongdu, capital of the preceding Liao and Jin dynasties (who, like the Mongols, had originated as Central Asian nomads). Construction began in 1272, the year after he assumed the Chinese name Yuan for his dynasty; it was inaugurated as the capital of the Mongol Empire in 1274. Here is Marco Polo's opening description of the city (illus. 29):

The entire exterior is a great square wall, a mile on
each side – that is to say it is four miles all around.
It is very thick and a good 10 paces high, all white
and crenellated. In each corner of this wall there is
a very beautiful and very rich palace, where the Great
Khan's equipment is kept: these are bows, quivers, saddles
and bridles for the horses, bowstrings, and everything
the army needs . . .

 This wall has five gates facing south: in the middle a
great gate that never opens except when the Great Khan
leaves or enters; beside this great gate there are two little
ones, one on each side; all other people enter through
these. Then there's another large one near one corner,
another near the other corner, through which other
people also enter. (§84, p. 74)

This rectilinear plan was instantly recognizable as the model set
by previous Chinese imperial capitals, based on ideals first artic-
ulated under the Zhou dynasty in the third century BCE. In fact,
Dadu consisted of walls within walls within walls. The innermost
set surrounded Qubilai's palace city, located in the eastern half
of a larger compound, the Imperial City, which included an artificial lake and the palaces of the dowager empress and the crown
prince. The Imperial City, in turn, was situated along the southern perimeter of the outermost city walls – an imposing structure
surrounded by a moat and made of pounded earth, nearly 30 kilometres (18 mi.) long, 8 metres (26 ft) high, 24 metres (78 ft) thick
at its base, tapering to 16 metres (52 ft) at its height. There were
eleven gates (three in the east, west and south walls, and two in
the north wall), each opening out onto a drawbridge spanning
the moat. The gates were connected by the primary thorough-
fares, perfectly oriented along north–south or east–west axes,
roughly 25 metres (82 ft) wide (the breadth of nine carriages);

these were intersected by secondary streets 6 or 7 metres (19 or 22 ft) wide.

To measure the impression such a city would have made on a young Marco Polo, one has only to think of his native city, 'ris[ing] out of the sea', with 'salt water run[ning] through it and around every place except in the houses and the streets', to return to the description by Martin da Canal that we quoted earlier (see also illus. 13). Nor could any of the walled cities of Western Europe boast anything similar: in Genoa, for example, where Marco and Rustichello of Pisa composed their *Description*, the twelfth-century walls, constrained by the topography of the coastal mountains on the one hand and the sea on the other, snaked irregularly around the city (illus. 30).

As physically imposing as this built environment was, for Marco Polo the merchant, the greatness of the capital was inseparable from the volume and variety of its trade:

> Know very truly that more costly and worthy things come to this city of Khanbaliq than to any city in the world . . . for I tell you that all the costly things coming from India – precious stones, pearls, and other costly things – are brought to this city; also, all the beautiful and most costly things from the province of Cathay and all other provinces are brought there. [G]reater quantities of the most costly and most worthy come to this city than to any city in the world; and more merchandise is sold and bought there; for know in truth that each day, more than 1,000 carts loaded with silk enter this city, for many cloths of gold and silk are produced there. (§95, pp. 85–6)

Strategically located for its access to the steppes in the north and to the China plain towards the south, Khanbaliq was intentionally constructed as the hub of Qubilai's empire. As Marco writes:

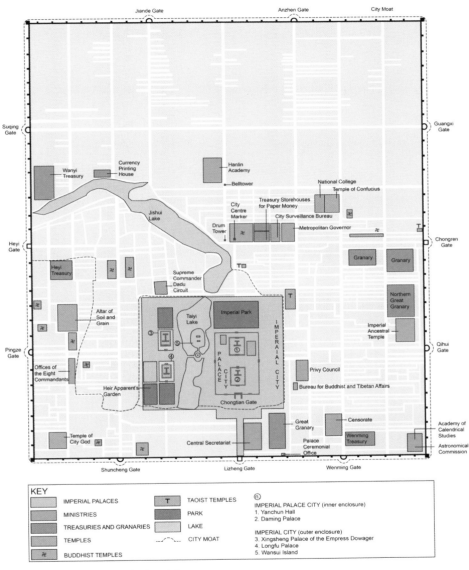

29 Plan of Khanbaliq (Dadu).

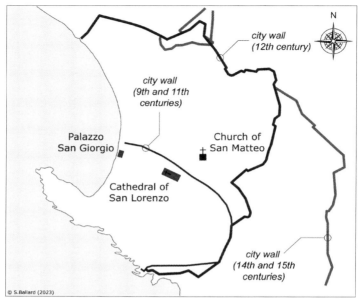

city wall
(12th century)

N

city wall
(9th and 11th
centuries)

Palazzo
San Giorgio

Church of
San Matteo

Cathedral of
San Lorenzo

city wall
(14th and 15th
centuries)

© S.Ballard (2023)

30 Map of Genoa.

'Now know in truth that many roads going to many provinces depart from this city of Khanbaliq: that is to say, one [road] goes to such-and-such a province and this [road] to another' (§98, p. 89). Alongside this network of roads, plied by travellers of all kinds and central to the system of post relays, the centripetal flow of goods to the capital was assured by its connectivity by water: not only its proximity to two rivers but by Qubilai's infrastructural projects repairing and extending the Grand Canal, facilitating the import both of grain to feed the population and of the commodities – 'precious stones, pearls, and other costly things' – that reached the ports of southern China from the maritime trade with South and Southeast Asia.

Like its rectilinear layout evoking past imperial capitals, Khanbaliq's connectivity by land and water was part of a concerted programme of empire that included the invention of a script, Phagspa, intended to record the multiple languages of

Qubilai's domain. The luxuries and commercial goods that Marco describes flowing into the city have a less practical, more symbolic parallel in the diverse flora and fauna that the Great Khan has assembled from as far as he can command. Within the bounds of the Imperial City, 'there are fields and beautiful trees, among which there are several kinds of different animals: white deer, the animals that make musk, roe deer, fallow deer, and two-toned squirrels, and several kinds of beautiful animals.' In the northwest corner of the compound, he continues, 'there's a very large lake in which there are many kinds of fish, for the great lord had many kinds of fish put there; and every time that the great lord wants some of these fish, he has as many as he desires' (§84, p. 74). Most ambitious of all is the Green Mound, an artificial hill constructed 'about a crossbow shot's length north of the palace' and surmounted by 'a large and beautiful palace that is completely green'. Around this structure, the mound

> is full of and covered with trees that never lose their
> leaves, but are always green. I tell you that wherever
> someone told the great lord about a beautiful tree,
> he had it taken up with all its roots and a lot of earth
> and had it carried to this mound by elephant . . . in
> this way, the most beautiful trees in the world were
> found there. (§84, p. 75)

Such assemblages of rare or unusual objects, commandeered by decree or received as gifts or as tribute, are recognizable expressions of imperial power, as in the zoological garden kept by Emperor Frederick ɪɪ (d. 1250) in his Sicilian capital of Palermo, which included a giraffe sent to him by the sultan of Egypt; or the treasury of the Fatimid sultans of Egypt (catalogued in a remarkable eleventh-century text called *The Book of Gifts and Rarities*) – forerunners of the Schatzkammers or cabinets of curiosities assembled by Renaissance princes. Of special note in the case of Qubilai's Green Mound is the practical use of elephants (captured in war or received as tribute) as beasts of burden rather than, as Marco Polo elsewhere describes, as props in his own performance of imperial power.

Importantly, Khanbaliq was the setting of the elaborate ceremonials convened by Qubilai – none more magnificent than his New Year's feast in the month of February. On that occasion, the entire court dressed in white, and provincial governors and tributary rulers brought the Great Khan 'very great presents of gold, silver, pearls, and precious stones, and many white cloths'. Thousands of white horses were presented to the ruler, and elephants and camels bedecked in rich embroidered cloths transported all the goods needed for the festivities. 'All pass before the great lord; it is the most beautiful sight to see ever seen' (§89, p. 70). In a highly choreographed ceremony, all the 'kings, dukes, marquis and counts, barons, knights, astronomers, physicians, falconers, and . . . other officials' in attendance bowed, 'putting their foreheads to the ground . . . direct[ing] their prayers toward the lord and worship[ping] him as if he were a god' (§89, p. 79). Qubilai then received gifts and offerings from his guests, followed by a banquet (liberally accompanied by drink) and courtly entertainment. Afterwards, 'everyone return[ed] to his lodging and his home', having ushered in the New Year in an auspicious manner by renewing their places in the good graces of the Great Khan.

Quinsai

A garden city located just one hour by high-speed train from the modern metropolis of Shanghai and touted in tourist literature as 'the Venice of the East', Quinsai (modern Hangzhou) in the thirteenth century was among the Old World's largest urban centres.[8] Under the name Lin'an, it had become the capital of the Southern Song (1127–1279) after its people were chased out of northern China by the Jin dynasty conquest (1127); fleeing south of the Yangtze River, the emperor settled in Hangzhou as his 'temporary residence' pending a reconquest of the north – a reconquest that never came. Originally, its picturesque landscape of hills and waterways served as added protection against the invaders, who (like the Mongols a century later) conducted their campaigns on horseback. Even before becoming the capital, it had served as an important port for overseas trade with Korea and Japan, as well as for the Persian and Arab ships coming from the Indian Ocean. Besides the many artisans and merchants it attracted, the influx of soldiers and bureaucrats linked to the imperial regime brought its population under the Southern Song to a peak of perhaps 1.5 million.

The same topographical features that made Hangzhou both picturesque and militarily defensible meant that it could not be laid out as a rectangular grid in the manner traditionally followed by earlier capitals such as Chang'an (§111, modern Xi'an) and eventually used, as we have seen, for Qubilai's new capital of Khanbaliq. The density of population within the resultingly constricted landscape also led to a proliferation of multi-storey buildings that lent it a vertical aspect. In contrast to the circumscribed blocks of earlier Chinese capitals but like the Northern Song capital of Kaifeng before it, Hangzhou featured open streets bristling with shops, restaurants, places of entertainment and specialized markets sprinkled throughout the city. Two centuries before Marco Polo, a Japanese monk visiting the city was struck by the night market,

> decorated with hundreds – thousands – of rare treasures. At one spot suspended in a row were two or three hundred glass lanterns . . . hung in front of every shop[,] colored green, red, or white. Some buildings were decorated with

jeweled curtains. Women strummed zitherns or played
flutes, and numerous masked performers were wonderfully
skilled. Also, water was used to make various dolls dance,
beat drums, or spout water. I cannot possibly describe all
their clever tricks.[9]

Spectacles such as these lent a beguiling aspect to what Marco
calls 'the best and the noblest city in the world' (§152, p. 133).

Under the Song, Hangzhou had lacked the sizeable communities of Arab and Persian merchants found in other great trading
emporia like Guangzhou or Quanzhou (Marco Polo's Zaytun).
The Mongol conquest of 1276 brought an influx of merchants –
primarily Muslim – from the Ilkhanate of Persia, then under the
rule of Qubilai's nephew Abaqa. 'Quinsai', Marco Polo's name
for the city, comes from 'Khinsai', the Persian rendering of the
Chinese xingzai (temporary capital) – the name from which our
word 'satin' ultimately derives. In 1281 a mosque (along with a
Nestorian temple) was built in the southern part of the city near
the ruins of the former imperial palace, at the heart of what would
become a flourishing commercial and entertainment district.

In the thirteenth century as today, Hangzhou's most distinctive feature was the body of water known as West Lake (illus. 31):

I also tell you that toward the south there is a lake, a good
30 miles around; and all around there are many beautiful
palaces and many beautiful houses belonging to nobles
and great men, so wondrously made that they could not
be better or more richly devised or done. There are
also many idolator abbeys and churches, in very great
quantities. I also tell you that, in the middle of the lake,
there are two islands, on each of which is a very wondrous
and rich palace, so well made and adorned that it quite
resembles an emperor's palace. When one wants to

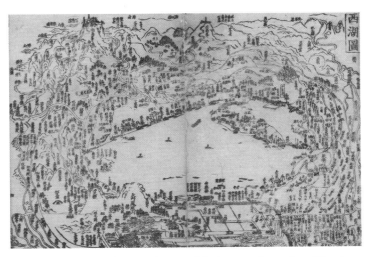

31 Wang Yao, *Map of West Lake*, woodblock printed map from *Xianchun Lin'an zhi* (Gazetteer of Lin'an, 1268–73).

hold a marriage or gathering, they go to this palace;
that's where they hold their marriages and feasts, and
everything needed for gatherings is found there – that
is, dishes, platters, and bowls. (§152, p. 134)

In the last days of the Southern Song, a minor official named
Dong Sigao composed a poetically innovative collection called
'One Hundred Poems on West Lake'; essentially a guided walking
tour around the lake, it departs from the Chinese tradition of
garden poetry to emphasize the site's empirical details and its role
as the hub of the bustling and socially diverse urban activity
around the capital. At about the same time, the distinctiveness
of the site was formalized into what would become a conventional
list of 'Ten Views' – some specific to a season or even a time of
day:

Autumn Moon above the Placid Lake, Spring Dawn at Su
Dike, Remnant Snow on Broken Bridge, Sunset on Leifeng

Pagoda, Evening Bell from Nanping Hill, Lotus Breeze at Qu Winery, Watching Fish at Flower Cove, Listening to the Orioles by the Willow Ripples, Three Stupas and the Reflecting Moon, and Twin Peaks Piercing the Clouds.[10]

This assembly of ten views inspired poetry: at least four collections of ten poems – several of which could function as miniature trip diaries – survive. It also inspired landscape paintings, which were sometimes paired with corresponding poems. In the 1280s, following the Mongol conquest of the Southern Song, the scholar and polymath Zhou Mi drew a colourful picture of the lake's built environment as the setting for Hangzhou's lively social scene (illus. 32):

> West Lake has the foremost scenery in the realm, perfect in the morning and the evening, in bright weather and in rain, and in all four seasons. The people of Hangzhou therefore roam the lake at every time of the year, although revelers are especially numerous during the spring . . . Here one may see the inhabitants of the capital contract marriages or celebrate the end of the year, gather with their families or send off the dead to be buried, discuss sutras or sacrifice to the gods. One may see arrangements for an appointment to an official post or for a bestowal of imperial grace, commissions by the imperial court or by the central government, noble eunuchs and prominent officials, great merchants and powerful persons, a companion bought for a thousand pieces of gold and gamblers staking a million. One may even see smitten lads and lovesick girls, and secret assignations and illicit gatherings.[11]

If Khanbaliq was defined by its walls, Quinsai, in Marco Polo's eyes, stood out for its bridges:

It is said that the city of Quinsai was about 100 miles around and had 12,000 stone bridges; as for each of these bridges, or for the majority, a great ship could easily pass beneath its arch; for the others, a smaller ship could. It's no marvel that there are so many bridges, for I tell you that this city is all on the water and is surrounded by water, and therefore it is fitting that there be many bridges for getting around the whole city. (§152, p. 133)

To fully appreciate the impression this cityscape would have made on Marco Polo, we have only to recall his native Venice. The Rialto Bridge, today one of the city's most iconic monuments, was not built in stone until the end of the sixteenth century; otherwise, the city's canals were spanned by wooden bridges lacking side rails. Tellingly, these are not the first bridges to have caught Marco Polo's attention. His description of the road leading out of Khanbaliq included 'a very beautiful stone bridge' over the Pulingsanggan River (illus. 33):

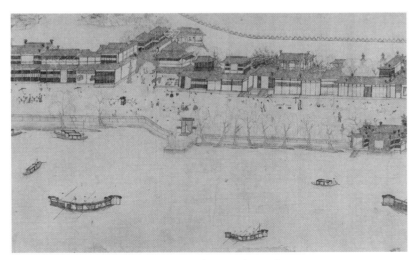

32 Unknown artist, *Scenic Attractions of West Lake*, 14th century, handscroll (detail), ink and colour on paper.

Know that in all the world there is no bridge as
beautiful or its like, and I will tell you how. I tell you
that it is a good 300 paces long and 8 wide: for 10 knights
side-by-side can easily cross it. There are 24 arches and
24 pillars in the water, all of grayish marble, well worked
and solidly set. On each side of the bridge is a wall of
marble panels and columns, made as I will tell you.
There is a marble column fixed at the head of the bridge,
and below the column a marble lion and atop the column
another beautiful, large, and well-made one. One and a
half paces from this column is another, identical one with
two lions; between one column and the other, a grayish
marble panel is fixed so that people don't fall in the water;
and thus it goes the whole length, such that it's really
a beautiful thing to see. (§105, p. 93)

Today dubbed the 'Marco Polo Bridge', the impression it made
on Marco could not be clearer from the length and detail of his
description.

Quinsai, as we recall, had come under Qubilai's rule only at
the close of the 1270s, when the Mongols completed their conquest of the Southern Song. The Polos, who had arrived in
Cathay (northern China) about a half-decade before, were thus
eyewitnesses to this world-historical moment, when imperial
China was reunified as it had not been for many centuries.
Quinsai, the Southern Song capital, was surely the jewel in the
crown of Qubilai's conquest. But a close second would have been
the magnificent port of Zaytun, to which we now turn.

Zaytun

The third of the great Chinese metropolises Marco Polo describes
is the city of Zaytun (modern Quanzhou). Situated on the straits
of Taiwan, it was a great commercial hub linking the maritime

33 Unknown artist, *Lugou Rafting Map*, 1206–1368, ink and colour on silk. The Lugou Bridge, or 'Marco Polo Bridge', is seen in the centre.

trade from South and Southeast Asia with land routes, both regional and long distance:

> In this city is the port where all the India ships come, with many commodities and luxuries, with many precious stones of great worth, and with many big, good-quality pearls. To this port come all the merchants of Mangi (which totally surrounds it); consequently, such a great abundance of commodities and stones come and go through this port that it's a marvelous thing to see; and from this city and port, they go throughout the entire province of Mangi. I tell you that for each shipload of pepper going to Alexandria or other places to be carried to Christian lands, a hundred come to this port of Zaytun, for you must know that this is one of the two ports in the world where the most merchandise comes from. (§157, p. 141)

Under earlier dynasties, Quanzhou had been favoured by rogue merchants seeking to evade customs duties at Guangzhou; in the late eleventh century, it superseded Guangzhou as the seat of a maritime trade superintendency. Goods imported by western Asian merchants were exchanged for an equal value of wares from official government stores. Since trade in metal, currency, weapons, wax, tea and other commodities was occasionally restricted, officials developed a market in ceramics produced expressly for export from both local and more distant production, as we will see later.

Under the Southern Song, Zaytun at first continued to prosper. In the late twelfth century, Zhao Rugua, the inspector of maritime trade, composed a work called the *Description of Barbarous Peoples* which combined a gazetteer of sites in the Indies, the Arabian Sea and even the distant Mediterranean with a catalogue of commodities like camphor, frankincense, nutmeg and pearls.

A shipwreck, dating from just before the Mongol conquest and excavated in 1974, offers a glimpse at the wealth of imports: aromatic woods like sandalwood and lakawood; medicinal products such as betel nut, frankincense, ambergris, cinnabar, mercury and tortoiseshell; and 5 litres (14 pt) of black pepper, helping to confirm Marco's assertion of the volume of that trade. The artefacts recovered by naval archaeologists revealed other details as well: wooden tags affixed to the cargo identifying its owners varied in shape according to the owners' rank. The ship's keel had holes at either end containing a bronze mirror and coins used as protective charms, arranged in a pattern with the constellation Ursa Minor above and a full moon below – a practice found in Fujian shipyards through the mid-twentieth century. In the meantime, however, piracy, compounded by the corruption of Southern Song officials, had put a damper on trade. The merchant community thus welcomed the Mongol conquest of 1279 – especially since taxes were reduced to half of what they were at the other six trade superintendencies.

All these trade connections made Zaytun a very cosmopolitan place. By the thirteenth century there were Muslim officials in the Southern Song government; by 1245–6 the trade superintendent was Pu Shougeng, likely a Muslim of Arab descent. In Marco Polo's time, the city and its environs had six mosques, endowed by Muslims from the Persian Gulf port of Siraf, Yemen, Tabriz (the Ilkhanid capital) and Khorazm; a Buddhist temple; Hindu temples devoted to Śiva and Vishnu, constructed in the thirteenth-century Dravidian style of the late Chola period; a Manichaean temple (later converted into a Buddhist shrine); and Christian, possibly Nestorian, tombstones. For most of Marco Polo's audience, accustomed to a Mediterranean landscape of Christian (Latin, Greek and various Orthodox churches), Muslim and Jewish communities, such religious diversity would have been beyond imagining – nearly as incomprehensible as the claim that 'for each shipload of pepper going to Alexandria or other places to be carried to Christian lands, a hundred come to this port of Zaytun.'

Seen through Marco Polo's eyes, the magnificence of these three great metropolises of Khanbaliq, Quinsai and Zaytun, each many times the size of any city in Latin Europe, would both have exemplified 'the diversities of the diverse regions of the world' (§1, p. 1) highlighted in Rustichello's opening lines and contributed to Marco's account of Qubilai as 'the most powerful in men, land, and treasure that the world has ever seen' (§76, p. 67). At the same time, their grandeur, as measured in their population, the extent of their city walls, the proliferation of stone bridges and the volume of their commerce, would have astonished their first audience, worthy of inclusion in a 'Book of Marvels', as we will take up in the following chapter.

THREE

The Book of Marvels

In comparison with the time-hallowed portrait which for so long constituted the agreed popular and general knowledge of the subject, Marco's Asia is strikingly deprived of wonders.
JOHN LARNER, *Marco Polo and the Discovery of the World*[1]

In 1413 John the Fearless, Duke of Burgundy, offered a magnificent New Year's present to his uncle John, Duke of Berry. As John was a noted bibliophile, remembered today for his celebrated book of hours, *Les Très Riches Heures du duc de Berry* (illus. 34), the gift was an illuminated manuscript, today housed in the French National Library in Paris. On its flyleaf, the duke's secretary wrote: 'This book is of the Marvels of the world (des Merveilles du monde) – that is, of the Holy Land, of the Great Khan, emperor of the Tartars and of the land of India.' Consisting of 299 folios (parchment leaves) and lavishly illustrated with 265 miniatures (illus. 35), its contents were effectively a compendium of travel narratives, including the Franciscan Odoric of Pordenone's account, composed in 1330, of his journey to India and China in the preceding decade, John Mandeville's fictional *Travels* (c. 1350s), and the Armenian prince Hetoum's *The Flower of Histories of the Lands of the East* (*La Fleur des histoires de la terre d'Orient*, 1307). But the very first text in this collection, occupying its initial 96 folios and featuring 84 miniatures, is 'Marco Polo's book of the Marvels of Greater Asia, Greater and Lesser

India and diverse regions of the world'. In a little over a century, the work that started as a description of the world had morphed into a description of its marvels.

A lot had happened in the century and more between Marco and Rustichello's original composition and the compilation of John of Berry's *Book of Marvels*. Most significant for our purposes, the Yuan dynasty, established by Qubilai in 1271, had been overthrown by the 'native' Chinese Ming dynasty in 1368. By the turn of the fifteenth century, the new players on the eastern Mediterranean and Asian political scene were the Ottomans, who had

34 Miniature from *Les Très Riches Heures du duc de Berry, c.* 1416.

35 The Polos meeting Qubilai Khan, miniature from Marco Polo,
Le Livre des merveilles, 1400–1420.

dealt a coalition of Western crusaders a disastrous defeat at the
Battle of Nicopolis (on the Danube in modern-day Bulgaria) in
1396, and Timur the Lame (d. 1405), the Central Asian conqueror
claiming descent from Chinggis Khan, whose conquests rivalled
those of Chinggis and his successors. Now, the version of Marco
Polo found in the *Livre des merveilles* was, like our Franco-Italian
Description, surprisingly devoid of marvels. Nevertheless, *merveilles*
provided a cultural concept capable of encompassing the wealth
of textual knowledge through which fifteenth-century Europeans
cumulatively thought about Asia. In this chapter, after a look at
the fascination that they exerted on the medieval world, we will
explore the particular spin that Marco Polo's *Description* gives to
the word and concept of 'marvel'.

Marvels in the Medieval World

Marvels were an abiding part of medieval culture. In the Western
tradition, *mirabilia* and *merveilles* were popular topics for books
and illuminations. A *Wonders of the World* (*Mirabilia mundi*),

طلعي ربذا به اذا به خلا فلاك ومقادير اجرام الكواكب وبعدها واقطارها واقطارها اذ لا يمكن لا يصعب

علي ذره به لم لمعلم الهندسه امر رجل الفاله المانع مرا و قلد مرسه نسهل عليه ان الارض الفطانته به و

فهر وكك ما ثمه ١٦ الطبعي العلك اسفل النور ان افضل النور من الشمس النور اشكال اختلافه ولونه المذا ابل كسو

كليج ليلت وملت ليله وتقطع جميع اتلاف ف شهر انه اصغر و بك ابن ملك وارتفعها ابرا ولذلك حتي ينتج النور هل

ببله شرا كمر المنازل الثانيه والعشرين يستقر ليله مان كان الشهر تسعه وعشرين شهر ليله ثم سهر وهمرب وا كأن

وا يبشر ليله تسع و عشرن و بقطع فا استشاره من لام عباد ان تشي مرى هلال كاكا انفال كا ا نحر بقدر تاه خال

بتي ادا لمرجون القديم بريد انه زل لكل ليله من كحم ما دخث اعين ادا نقدم وبرق و ا يستنفي

وا ان ببم الغر جز جز تسعه وخمس جز اهم جم و مرجم الارض و دونه د ونه اربعانه واثنا و خمسون منها لا

طجم الغز ثانيه واربعه واربعه واربعون ميلا با نقرب منها وصل اليه ادرا القوم بجسر الفده ا ثنا ليجا بله به

اعلم ا نصبه لته فض زياده ضوا الغز ونقصانه الغرجم ثمت اعظم

لتبا ا ١٢ ا دبل منه علا يارى يظا هرانا لنصف يواجهه الشمس ضي ابرا ان ذا انارا اتشرق كل الم نصف

لط مواجها لتشرب ل المشرق وعمال النصف لمطار لجانب التي الي المغرب الي الارض يظهر نصف الصف

روي الجه لكال كما را سابل لانحرات و بردا د بترايع التقطع من النصف المضا لضي حتي اذا نا به د مقا بله ا نشر

النصف المضا لواجه لتنس هوا ا لتصا ل ل مواجهه نا ثم يقرب بن اتنر يتقرب فيبعض اصبا ر بن الجابب

وهو بعد بسيط فلك ان كان بين ثابتين من بعدهما مركبة العالم البسيط الأعلى عليهما لمتغير فلك عطارد والأولاد الحجر...

(الأسطر التالية من النص العربي)

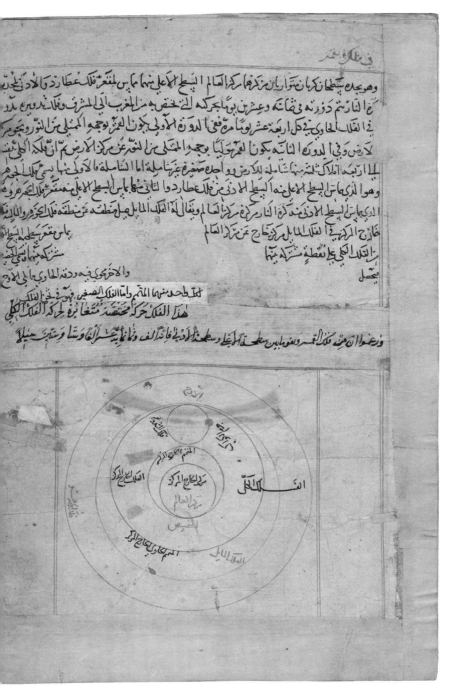

37 Miniature from al-Qazwīnī, *The Wonders of Creation*, c. 1300.

for example, features in a luxury manuscript (Los Angeles, the J. Paul Getty Museum, MS Ludwig XV 4) produced in 1277 or after in Thérouanne, in a workshop that also produced a lavish copy of Brunetto Latini's *Book of the Treasure* (Paris, BNF MS Français 567) at about the same time.[2]

Belief in miracles, in saints as intercessors, and in the power of relics was fundamental to the Christian Middle Ages. In his *Chronicle of the City of Genoa*, Archbishop Jacopo da Varagine reports that in the year 1230, after two of the four pirates sentenced to public execution in the piazza of San Lorenzo commended themselves to the relics of St John the Baptist (housed in the adjacent cathedral), they survived the initial attempt at hanging and were subsequently pardoned. From his own tenure in office, one of the events he describes at length is the opening of a marble sarcophagus located above the altar of the cathedral that was purported to contain the body of St Syrus; to counter doubts that had arisen, 'we had the tomb opened in the presence of the council and the podestà, the *capitano*, the abbot of the people, and many other nobles of the city of Genoa.' The bones and accompanying texts found in the sealed wooden casket succeeded in quelling previous doubts; Jacopo ordered the bones and the epitaph to be displayed to the people for the saint's feast day: 'and they were viewed by all with the greatest devotion and venerated humbly.'[3] Relics were objects not only of spiritual devotion but of intense civic pride.

Interest in marvels was likewise widespread in the Islamic tradition. In circa 1260–80, the decades following Hülegü Khan's overthrow of the Abbasid caliphate, a judge (*qadi*) and legal scholar named Zakariyya ibn Muhammad al-Qazwīnī (d. 1283) composed a work entitled *The Wonders of Creation and the Oddities of Existing Things* (*Ajā'ib al-makhlūqāt wa gharā'ib al-mawjūdāt*). Hailing from Qazvin (one of Marco Polo's '8 kingdoms' of Persia, northwest of present-day Tehran), Qazwīnī fled a Mongol massacre in 1220; he found refuge in Mosul, studying philosophy there before finally settling in Wasit (on the Tigris River), a thriving centre for book production, where he rode out Hülegü's conquest of 1258. Two early manuscripts of the *Wonders of Creation* overlap exactly with the period of Marco Polo's Asian travels and Genoese captivity: the first, produced in Wasit in 1280 (illus. 36) for the author himself; the second made in Mosul circa 1300 (illus. 37). These manuscripts have attracted the attention of art historians for their vivid illustrations; early examples of the florescence of book arts that followed the Mongol conquest of Persia, they preserve the text that in many ways inaugurated and set the template for the ongoing genre of 'The Wonders of Creation'.

Foreign Lands and Everyday Wonders

Rustichello's prologue, as we have seen, opens with the promise to reveal to its audience 'all the greatest marvels (*merveilles*) and great diversities of Greater Armenia, Persia, the Tartars, India, and many other provinces' (§1, p. 1). From the outset, that is, marvels are paired with diversity, the book's abiding obsession. This link is reinforced a few pages later, in the account of the elder Polos' first journey to the court of Qubilai Khan: 'They found great marvels and diverse things.' That these are the main attraction of the *Description* is evident from the way Rustichello strategically withholds them in order to command his audience's continued attention: 'We won't tell you about them here since Messer Marco, Messer Niccolò's son, who also saw all these things, will tell them to you clearly farther on in this book' (§5, p. 5).

The first objects of wonder in the book are in fact the elder Polos themselves. Prevented from returning home by the wars between the khanate of the Golden Horde and the Ilkhanate, the brothers plunge deeper into Central Asia, eventually reaching the famed Silk Road city of Bukhara. When they had been there for three years, the prologue recounts:

> there came an envoy from [the Ilkhan] Hülegü, lord
> of the East, on his way to the great lord of all the Tartars,
> named Qubilai. When this messenger saw Messer Niccolò
> and Messer Maffeo, he greatly marveled, for they had
> never seen any Latin in this country. (§4, p. 4)

Strikingly, this vignette challenges expectations by reversing our point of view: instead of looking at the wonders and curiosities of foreign lands through Venetian eyes, we instead see the Polos through Mongol eyes. On the Polos' second voyage, this reversal also encompasses the young Marco, who 'learned the Tartars' customs, languages, and writing so well that it was a marvel' (§16, p. 10). Moreover, when the Great Khan expresses frustration at the 'fools and ignoramuses' who return from far-away places unable to say anything about 'the news and the customs and practices' of the lands they have visited, Marco takes note and consequently 'put a good deal of effort into being able to tell the

Great Khan all about the novelties and strange things' he had seen (§16, p. 10). As a result, on returning to court he spoke 'so well and intelligently that the Great Khan and everyone who heard him marveled, saying to each other: if this young man lives a long life, he will surely become a man of great intelligence and great worth' (§17, p. 11). More than two decades before his collaboration with Rustichello, it is precisely by observing and describing the wonders of the world for the benefit of the Great Khan that Marco first marks himself out as a wonder.

The early chapters of the *Description* proper feature several examples of the place-based marvels of nature typical of medieval travel narratives, like Gerald of Wales's late twelfth-century accounts of Wales and Ireland. In the kingdom of Georgia, a mountain lake beside 'a monastery of nuns' called Saint Leonard teems with fish during Lent but at no other times of the year (§23, p. 18). In the desert of Lop in remote Central Asia – a desolate place with brackish water and no animals or birds – a traveller who gets separated from his companions

> hear[s] spirits talking in a way that seems to be his companions: for sometimes they call them by name. Many times they cause them to stray in such a way that they are never found; in this way, many have died and been lost. I also tell you that men hear these spirit voices even during the day, and often it seems like you hear many instruments – that is, drums – being played.
> (§57, pp. 44–5)

As striking as they are, such phenomena remain rare in the *Description*, in which the majority of geographical entries formulaically register ruler, religion, language and major commodities (natural or manufactured) of the cities and provinces across the Mongol Empire and beyond.

Marco does, however, show an abiding interest in the spells and divinations wrought by various 'enchanters'. There are the idolators of Kashmir who 'know so many devilish enchantments that it's a marvel: for they make their idols talk' (§49, p. 39) and the astronomers and wise enchanters who disperse bad weather from around the Great Khan's palace (§75, p. 65). One exception that proves the rule is his account of the 'wisest magicians and the best astronomers' found in Tibet, who 'through the diabolical arts . . . perform the strongest spells and the greatest marvels to hear about and to see, which are not good to relate in our book because people would marvel too much'. Dismissing these enchanters' 'evil customs', the narrative shifts back to the more mundane mention of their mastiffs and lanner falcons for hunting (§116, p. 102).

Often lost amid the *Description*'s account of the Mongols and other foreign people and places is how much Marco marvels at animals. In describing southwestern Cathay, he says, 'I will tell you a marvel: for I tell you that in this region, there are dogs so bold that they will attack lions' (§130, p. 116). The province of Tangut features 'wild cattle as big as elephants, very beautiful to see, for they are hairy (except on their back) and are white and black . . . so beautiful that it's a marvel to see' (§72, pp. 60–61). On the Qaramoran (Yellow) River, 'There is such a great multitude of birds that it's a marvel, for you can get three pheasants for one Venetian groat' (§110, p. 96). In Qarajang (the kingdom of Dali in the modern Chinese province of Yunnan) are 'great serpents . . . so exceedingly large that all men must marvel': ten paces long and ten palms around, they have 'a nail like that of a falcon or a lion' and a mouth 'so large that it could well swallow a man whole' (§119, p. 105). That Rustichello uses 'nail' to describe what we recognize as the claw of a crocodile is a reminder both of the limits of his Old French vocabulary and of the novelty of many of the things Marco Polo describes. East Africa abounds in remarkable fauna. In Mogadishu (on the Somali coast), 'There are different birds – that is, different from ours – which is a marvel' (§191, p. 181). Marco reports that messengers returning from an embassy of the Great Khan 'related many great marvels to the Great Khan about these strange islands' and brought back 'wild boar teeth . . . large beyond measure, including one that weighed 14 pounds' (§191, pp. 181–2). Of al-Shihr (on the southern coast of the Arabian peninsula), after describing the sheep there as 'beautiful little animals', Marco pauses:

> I also tell you something that will seem a marvel to you, for know in all truth that their animals – that is, sheep, oxen, camels, and their little packhorses – eat fish, and that is their food, for there is no grass in all their land or all their country . . . it is the driest place in the world.

Here as elsewhere the formulaic phrases 'I also tell you' and 'know in all truth' doubly reinforce the sense of wonder that this bizarre example should inspire. Moreover, 'the fish that the animals eat are very little and are caught in March, April, and May in such great quantities that it is a marvel' (§195, p. 189). Even animal marvels, however, accrue to the credit of the Great Khan, as on the borders of Mongolia, where he orders aviaries housing a 'very great number of cators, which we call great partridges . . . such a great quantity that it's a marvel to behold' (§74, p. 63). Finally, the great feasts held in Khanbaliq feature an amazing spectacle:

> I will also tell you a thing that seems a marvel, which is worth mentioning in our book: for know that a great lion is brought before the great lord; and as soon as the lion sees him, he throws himself down before him and shows great humility, seeming to recognize him as lord. He stays

before him with no chain and this is something to marvel
at. (§90, pp. 80–81)

For Marco the merchant, the world of commerce and artisanal
production is just as likely as the natural world to inspire wonder.
In the Persian province of Kerman (under Ilkhanate rule):

> Their ladies and maidens nobly ply their needles on silk
> cloths of all colors, making animals, birds, and many other
> images. So well do they work the hangings for barons and
> lords that it's a marvel to see; they also do very delicate
> work on coverlets, cushions, and pillow covers. (§35, p. 28)

In Cathay, the people of Dongpingfu (in western Shandong province) 'have such an abundance of silk that it's a marvel' (§134,
p. 118). The river running through Xinzhou 'carries such a great
abundance of merchandise to Mangi and through Cathay that it's
a marvel'. Marco further underscores that the ships sail fully loaded
in both directions: 'Therefore it is a marvelous thing to see the
merchandise carried upstream and downstream by this river'
(§135, p. 119). In Mangi (the recently conquered Southern Song
empire), the salt revenue accruing to the Great Khan from the
port of Quinsai is a marvel (§153, p. 137), while the 'great abundance of commodities and stones' that come and go through the
port of Zaytun is 'a marvelous thing to see' (§157, p. 141).

Mongols and Marvels

Connecting the titles *The Book of Marvels* and *The Book of the
Great Khan* is the fact that many of the *Description*'s greatest
marvels concern the Mongols and their empire, beginning with
their astonishing rise to power in the early years of the thirteenth
century:

Chinggis Khan held the lordship nobly and well. What should I tell you? Such a multitude of Tartars came to him that it was a marvel; and when Chinggis Khan saw that he had so many people, he equipped them with bows and armor and went conquering through those other lands. (§65, p. 52)

Here, the 'marvel' concerns the scale on which Chinggis is able to muster his warriors. Further on, it is the strangeness of the Mongols' customs or practices themselves:

Know in truth that all the great lords descended from the lineage of Chinggis Khan are taken for burial to a great mountain called Altai. Wherever the great lords die, if they die within a 100 days' journey of this mountain, they are taken there for burial. I tell you another marvel . . . (§69, p. 55)

For Westerners, whose rulers were typically interred in a cathedral or other sacred site at the heart of their kingdom or province, this distant burial place – so secret that efforts to locate Chinggis's tomb continue to pop up in the news to this day – would have seemed surpassingly strange. Elsewhere, it is the Mongols themselves who experience wonder in the course of their campaigns of conquest. After Qubilai's brother Hülegü took Baghdad in 1258, he found the Abbasid caliph cowering in 'a tower full of gold, silver, and other treasure – such that never had so much been seen in a single place at one time', provoking his wonder that this massive wealth had not been put to use to hire mercenaries to defend his city (§25, p. 20).

Battles are occasions for marvels – not, as we might expect, for the heroism of the combatants or for instances of divine intervention (as is the case in some Western Crusade chronicles and epic songs), but for their size and scale. In Qubilai's clash against his rebellious cousin Nayan, 'so many men died on both sides that it was a marvel to see' (§79, p. 70). When the Mongols' horses are spooked by the opponent's war elephants in a campaign against the Burmese kingdom of Pagan, they 'shot so many arrows that it was a marvel' (§123, p. 111). Setting the scene for the confrontation between Qubilai's son and Qaidu, another rebellious cousin, Marco says: 'I tell you that both these peoples were drawn up, awaiting the battle and the sounding of the drums, they sang and played so well it was a marvel to hear' (§199, p. 195). And, in the final chapter of the *Description*, when rival claimants to the khanate of the Golden Horde engage in battle, 'There was such a multitude of [arrows] that it was a marvel to see and it seemed like rain' (§232, p. 222).

As befits a work with the alternate title *The Book of the Great Khan*, however, many of the *Description*'s marvels cluster around Qubilai himself. His palace in Khanbaliq has 'so many chambers that it's a marvel to see; it is so large and well made that no man in the world, if he had the power, would be able to design or build it better' (§84, p. 74). Other marvels associated with the Great Khan include the number of people attending his seasonal hunting encampment and the skilfully wrought halls of his pavilion, lined with furs of ermine and sable (§94, p. 84).

Some of the text's most effusive language, however, concerns the Southern Song empire – Marco Polo's 'Mangi' – not completely subdued until after the Polos' arrival at Qubilai's court. It was impressive even by Mongol standards; as Marco puts it, 'this was quite a great conquest: there was no kingdom in the whole world worth half as much as this one, for the king had so much at his disposal that it was a marvelous thing' (§139, p. 124). Qubilai's new possession was vast on a scale unimaginable in Europe or the Mediterranean, as highlighted by Marco's emphatic formulations: 'I will also tell you something over which you will greatly marvel:

for I tell you that in the province of Mangi there are a good 1,200 cities; the Great Khan has a guard in each one' (§152, p. 135). It elicits wonder not just, as here, for its quantifiable wealth but for its quality and splendour; in the former imperial palace at Quinsai, 'The hall is completely decorated and painted with good paintings; there are many stories and many animals, birds, knights, ladies, and other marvels; it's a very beautiful sight to see, for on all the walls and all the ceilings you could see nothing but gold paintings' (§152, p. 136). Palaces in general excite Marco's attention. In his chapter on Japan, which he is unlikely to have seen at first hand, he writes:

> I will tell you a great marvel about a lord's palace on this island: I tell you in complete truth that there is a very large palace which is all covered with pure gold; just in the way that we cover our houses and our churches with lead, just so is this palace covered in pure gold, which is worth so much that it can hardly be told. (§159, p. 144)

We will return to some of the other marvels of Asia in a moment. But alongside these wonders associated with the splendour of imperial rule, we also find miracle stories of holy figures – like those told in canonical collections from the Latin West, but with a difference.

Miracles and the Sacred

Jacopo da Varagine, the archbishop of Genoa during Marco and Rustichello's captivity, is best remembered today as the author of *The Golden Legend* (*Legenda Aurea*), a compendium of saints' lives and Christian doctrine (the latter linked to expositions on feast days) intended as a handbook for preachers. Composed in the 1260s, this compilation – typical of the encyclopaedic impulse that characterized the thirteenth century – drew on a wide range of sources: the Gospels, the Old Testament book of Psalms and book of Isaiah, the Pauline epistles, the Acts of the Apostles, patristic writers, lives of the Desert Fathers and even collections made by some of his fellow Dominicans earlier in the century. In his choice of saints, he heavily favoured traditional figures from the early years of Christianity over holy men and women from closer to his own time. *The Golden Legend* became a medieval bestseller, with copies proliferating in Latin and in vernacular translations even in its author's lifetime.[4] Given both its popularity and its rather conservative hue, it is tempting to imagine Marco and Rustichello in captivity, perhaps within a stone's throw of Jacopo's archiepiscopal palace, methodically recording versions of the lives of some of the same saints contained in *The Golden Legend*, but with a defamiliarizing, distinctly Asian, twist.

St Thomas

Jacopo da Varagine's account of St Thomas the Apostle opens by exploring possible etymologies of his name: it may come from a word meaning twofold, he writes, 'because he came to know the Lord's resurrection in two ways – not only by sight, like the others, but by seeing and touching'; or from a word meaning dividing or separating, because 'he set himself apart from the other disciples by not at first believing that Christ had risen' – an allusion to the story of 'doubting' Thomas from the Gospel of John.[5] Thomas's wanderings begin when an emissary from an Indian king arrives in Caesaria in search of an architect to build him a palace in the Roman style; though Thomas is reluctant, God orders him to go, promising that once he has converted the Indians, 'you shall come to me with the palm of martyrdom.' Once in India, Thomas falls afoul of the king by failing to build his earthly palace, using the money instead to give alms to the poor; nevertheless, he eventually succeeds in converting first the king's brother (who dies and is brought back to life), followed by the king himself. Preaching to the poor and curing the sick, lame and feeble, he baptizes thousands of new Christians, and the miracles he performs win him fame throughout Upper India. Thomas meets his martyrdom at the court of another king: having persuaded the king's wife and sister-in-law to live chastely with their husbands, he is subjected to a series of punishments and trials, including being ordered to worship the king's 'hand-made idol'. Invoking the name of Jesus Christ, he commands the demon inside the idol to destroy it, causing it to melt 'as if it were made of wax'. In fury, the temple's high priest runs Thomas through with a sword. His Christian followers carry his body away and gave it an 'honorable burial'. Two centuries later, in the reign of Emperor Severus Alexander, his body was transferred to Edessa (in Upper Mesopotamia), helping to safeguard the city from its enemies.

In *The Golden Legend* as elsewhere, Thomas is the saint most closely associated with India. In contrast to Jacopo's account, however, Marco's embeds him in a precise geography: he locates the body of 'Messer Saint Thomas the Apostle' in Maabar, the medieval Arabic name for the Coromandel coast of southeastern India – more specifically, in a small town unfrequented by merchants, 'for there is no merchandise that can be exported and, what's more, the place is very out of the way'. Nevertheless, the place draws pilgrims – not just Christians but 'many Saracens', for 'the Saracens of this country have great faith in him; they say that he was Saracen and that he is a great prophet, and they call him *avarian*, which means "holy man".' (Such shared sacred spaces, reflecting the common Abrahamic roots of Christianity and Islam, were common across the premodern world.) One 'marvel' (*mervoie*) associated with the site is its red earth, which, when mixed with water and drunk, cures quartan, tertian or other fevers and is thus highly prized by pilgrims. In addition, 'all year, a lot of other miracles [*miracles*] occurred that would well be held in "great wonder" [*grant meraveies*] by whoever heard them told – especially the curing of Christians who are crippled and wasted in body' (§176, p. 164).

The centrepiece of Marco's chapter, however, is a 'fine miracle' (*biaus miracle*) dated to 1288 – only half a decade before the Polos traversed this region on their homeward journey to Venice. A local 'idolatrous baron' had filled the pilgrims' lodgings around the church with 'a great quantity of the grain called rice'. The shrine's guardians prayed to St Thomas, who responded with a 'great miracle':

> For know that the night after this baron had had the
> houses filled, Messer Saint Thomas appeared to him
> with a fork in hand, put it to the baron's throat, and said:
> 'O so-and-so, if you don't empty my houses immediately,
> it will be fitting that you die an evil death.' While he was
> saying this, he pushed his neck with this fork so hard that
> the baron thought himself in great pain and in danger of
> death; and when my lord Saint Thomas had done this, he
> left. This baron immediately got up and had all these
> houses emptied out and recounted all that my lord Saint
> Thomas had done to him, which was easily held to be
> a great miracle. The Christians were very joyful and
> very happy and paid great thanks and great honor to
> Messer Saint Thomas and repeatedly blessed his name.
> (§176, p. 164)

Overtly, this episode highlights a conflict between a local lord and a religious minority community under his rule. At the same time, it evokes Marco's account of the grain stockpiled by Qubilai Khan in times of surplus, to be redistributed to his people in times of famine. What's the difference? Were local rice farmers resisting levies of their crops? Or rebelling against a lord perceived to be hoarding grain instead of distributing it? While the context behind this miracle story is impossible to recover, St Thomas's physical intimidation of a lord who had expropriated part of his shrine shows a resolution of the kind of socio-historical entanglements that could arise between local religious and secular leaders in favour of the former.

As for the martyrdom of the saint himself, in Marco's telling, his death at the hands of an enraged idolator priest is recast as a random hunting accident. One day while Thomas was praying outside his hermitage, an idolator

> let fly an arrow from his bow to kill one of the peacocks around the saint. He didn't see him at all, and thinking he had hit the peacock, he hit Messer Saint Thomas the Apostle in the right side. When he received this hit, he very softly prayed to his Creator and I tell you that he died of this blow. (§176, p. 165)

On the one hand, this accidental shooting seems to deny the saint the crown of martyrdom; on the other hand, the arrow wound in his side vividly evokes Christ's wound probed (according to the Gospel of John) by the incredulous apostle, thus lending allegorical weight to an otherwise anticlimactic incident. Where *The Golden Legend* and the *Description* do agree is on the expansive geography of St Thomas's mission. Jacopo cites the seventh-century bishop Isidore of Seville on his preaching to 'the Parthians, the Medes, and Persians, the Hircanians, and the Bactrians', and the fourth-century Church Father John Chrysostom on the conversions the saint made in 'the land of the Magi'.[6] This largely corresponds with the version found in Brunetto Latini's *Book of the Treasure* (written in French in the

1260s), which has St Thomas preaching 'in Persia, in Media and in Hyrcania, and in India towards the east. In the end he was wounded with swords and lances, and he died 11 days before the end of December in a city of India named Calamina; and he was buried there honorably.'[7] The *Description* modifies and expands this geography, adding that St Thomas 'converted many people in Nubia' (§176, p. 165); this association with East Africa recurs in a later chapter on 'Abyssinia', the land Marco calls 'Middle India' (§193, p. 184).

In 1321, within Marco Polo's lifetime, the martyrdom of four Franciscan missionaries in the South Asian port of Tana (on the west coast, just northwest of modern Mumbai) would give added resonance to tales of the death of St Thomas. In the *Description*, by contrast, the violence surrounding a Christian figure, however vividly told, is safely sequestered in the time of the apostles, while a more contemporary confrontation is resolved in the favour of the local Christian community.

From Sergamoni Borcan to Sts Barlaam and Josaphat

If the shrine of St Thomas honours a holy figure revered by followers of two different religions, Christianity and Islam, Marco's account of the island of Sarandib (Ceylon, present-day Sri Lanka) highlights a mountain sacred to followers of two different religions, Islam and Buddhism, as the burial place of two different holy figures: 'Adam our first father' for Muslims; and 'Sergamoni Borcan', the Mongol name for the Buddha (Sakyamuni), for 'idolators'. Leaving its association with Adam to the side (in Christian tradition, he is buried in Jerusalem), Marco takes up the story of the latter – the prince who grows up carefully shielded from all hardship; upon discovering the outside world of death and old age, he leaves his sheltered life in order to retreat to a 'faraway mountain'. There 'he remained his whole life, simply and chastely, practicing great abstinence. Had he been Christian,' this account concludes, 'he would have been a great saint with our lord Jesus Christ' (§178, p. 169).

In Marco Polo's day this story was already well known, but as the legend of the Christian saints Barlaam and Josaphat. In a remarkable chain of transmission crossing multiple languages, religions and cultures, the original Sanskrit life of the Buddha was translated first into Persian, then into Arabic under the title *The Book of Bilawhar and Būdhāsaf* (c. 750–900). This version was translated into Georgian and Christianized under the title *Balavariani*; then translated into Greek in the early eleventh century; then translated multiple times from Greek into Latin, beginning in the mid-eleventh century. The Latin tale was translated into French several times, first in the twelfth century, then in the 1220s in an extended version by Gui de Cambrai (also the author of a short episodic epic belonging to the Alexander Romance tradition); in the same decade, Rudolf von Ems (also author of a *World Chronicle* and an *Alexander Romance*) made a translation into Middle High German. By the time Marco and Rustichello composed the *Description*, Barlaam and Josaphat had become a pan-Eurasian phenomenon.

The Latin version incorporated into Jacobus of Voragine's *Golden Legend*, set in a time when 'all India was teeming with Christians and monks' (presumably reflecting the success of St Thomas's mission), opens with 'a certain very powerful king named Avennir' who came to power and began persecuting the Christians. When one of the astrologers summoned to celebrate the birth of Avennir's son Josaphat predicts that the prince will not reign after his father but instead 'will worship as a believer in Christ's religion, which you are persecuting!', the king has Josaphat secluded in a fine palace and shielded from the ills of the world, making sure that 'not a word about Christ was ever to be spoken to the royal child.' As a young man, however, Josaphat is disturbed to meet a leper and a blind man and to learn about old age and death. A Christian monk named Barlaam seeks him out and relates a series of parables illustrating why he should shun worldly treasures and embrace a life of virtuous simplicity that will lead to the greater reward of heaven. Barlaam baptizes Josaphat but dissuades him from returning to the desert with him, telling him to bide his time. Back at court, the king tries various ruses to lure his son away from Christianity, including a religious disputation between a false Barlaam and a court theologian, and a sorcerer's plot to seduce Josaphat with a bevy of beautiful women. The greatest temptation of all is a king's daughter, who enjoins him:

> if you wish to save my soul, grant me one tiny petition: lie with me tonight, that's all, and I promise you I will become a Christian! For if, as you say, there is joy before the angels of God over one sinner who repents, is not a great reward due the one who brings about the conversion? Just do what I want this one time, and so you will save me!

Reduced to tears, Josaphat is saved by a dream that reveals the evil behind this scheme, and he ends by converting the sorcerer.

Unable to deter his son from a life of piety, Avennir bestows half his kingdom on him. Josaphat accepts 'in order to spread the Christian faith'; during his brief reign, he erects churches and converts all his people to Christ – including, eventually, his father, who 'devoted himself to good works and finished his life virtuously'. Josaphat then resigns his kingship and flees to the desert; evading the many traps the Devil sets for him, he spends two years searching for Barlaam until they are joyously reunited.

> Josaphat lived there for many years in marvelous austerity and virtue. Barlaam ended his days in peace about A.D. 380. Josaphat, having abdicated his throne at the age of

twenty-five, lived the life of a hermit for thirty-five years, until, adorned with many virtues, he died in peace and was laid to rest beside Barlaam's body.

The ruler to whom Josaphat had ceded his kingdom has both bodies brought back to the city, where 'many miracles have occurred at their tomb'.

Though the story of the Christian saints Barlaam and Josaphat was well known in the West in both Latin and French, Marco Polo's version relates the life of 'Sergamoni Borcan', 'the first man [the idolators] held holy and in whose name they made idols' (§178, p. 169). The story of the Buddha is told in two episodes: his imperviousness to the temptation of being surrounded by 30,000 'very beautiful and comely' maids; and his realization of the transitoriness of life after seeing a dead man and old man – the encounter that leads him to abandon the world for the life of an ascetic, not in a desert but on 'some great, faraway mountains'. There is no Barlaam figure to teach or model the virtues of a holy life. Rather, the tale highlights the perspective of the prince's father: when he saw that his son 'wanted nothing to do with earthly power, he got so angry that he almost died of affliction. And no wonder: for this was his only son, and he had no one to whom to leave his kingdom.' And after Sergamoni's death, it is the king who makes him into an idol.

> When he saw that the one he loved more than himself
> was dead, you needn't ask if he was vexed and distressed:
> he mourned greatly, and had a likeness made of pure gold
> and precious stones, and had all his subjects honor and
> worship him as a god. (§178, p. 169)

As in the case of Thomas the Apostle, Marco's primary interest remains the pilgrimage site, which brings him back to its contested history: 'I tell you truly that idolaters come on pilgrimage from very distant parts, just as Christians go on pilgrimage to Messer Saint James'. At the same time, 'the Saracens, who also come on pilgrimage here in great numbers, say that this is the monument of Adam our first father.' Both sides claim the site's relics – teeth, hair and a bowl – as having belonged to their revered figure. Having at first de-exoticized the idolaters' pilgrimage by likening it to the Christian site of Santiago de Compostela in the northwesternmost corner of the Iberian peninsula (one of the four great pilgrimage sites of the Middle Ages, along with Jerusalem, Rome and Canterbury), Marco concludes with this disclaimer: 'But God knows who he is and who he was, for we do not believe that Adam is here in this place, because the Scripture of the Holy Church says that he's in another part of the world' (§178, p. 169).

For Marco, however, the tale's ultimate significance lies in the interest that the relics arouse in Qubilai Khan. As he tells it, when the Great Khan heard about them, 'he said to himself it was fitting that he should have them.' So in the year 1284 he sent a great embassy that importuned the local king so much that he granted them 'the two molars, which were fat and large . . . the hairs, and the bowl . . . of very beautiful green porphyry . . . understood to be Adam's'. In Khanbaliq the relics are received 'with great joy, celebration, and reverence'. Marco adds:

> I tell you that they found in their writings that this bowl had such properties that if you filled it with food enough for one man, there would be enough for 5; and the Great Khan said that he had tested it, and that it was true.
>
> In such a way as you have heard, the Great Khan got the relics that you've heard about. It cost him quite a great amount of treasure to acquire them. (§178, pp. 170–71)

In short, relics of the Buddha, from a distant sacred space shared with Islamic traditions of Adam, are uprooted and transmitted to Qubilai's court, centripetally pulling them into the Mongol orbit worthy of mention in the *Book of the Great Khan*. Like the 'translation' (as the transfer of medieval relics is called) of the body of St Mark from Alexandria to Venice, the expropriation of the Buddha's teeth, hair and bowl both symbolizes and exalts the power of Qubilai and his capital.

Other miracle stories that Marco and Rustichello relate are set within living memory. The first 'great marvel' concerns 'a caliph who wished very great ill on the Christians' who devises a plan to bring about their conversion or death (§26, p. 21). Invoking a passage from gospel (Matthew 17:20) about the power of faith to move mountains, he challenges local Christians to move a nearby mountain on pain of death. In an extended narrative spun out over four chapters (§§26–9), the Christians locate a one-eyed shoemaker renowned for his piety (having put his own eye out when tempted by the shapely leg of a woman he had been fitting for shoes) and whose prayer succeeds in moving the mountain.

> When the caliph and the Saracens saw this, they greatly marveled and several of them turned Christian. And the caliph himself became Christian, but in secret: except that, when he died, a cross was found around his neck; so the Saracens didn't bury him in the tomb of the other caliphs, but put him in another place. (§29, p. 24)

This story of Christian triumph closely parallels a miracle found in an eleventh-century Coptic Christian source set in tenth-century Cairo. In Marco's version the Christians in question are 'Nestorian and Jacobite' (§26, p. 21) – members of two eastern churches widespread across Asia but whose divergences from Latin Christianity had shocked and scandalized the Franciscan

William of Rubruck during his 1253–5 embassy to the Mongols, as recorded in his report to King Louis IX of France.[8] Most strikingly, Marco sets the event in 1275, two decades after the year in which, as he had described in the preceding chapter, Hülegü Khan had put the last caliph to death: 'After this caliph, there was no longer a caliph' (§25, p. 21). Whether wittingly or inadvertently, Marco and Rustichello set the miracle of the mountain moved by the prayer of the one-eyed shoemaker in an impossible time of chronological contradiction.

A second Christian miracle takes place in the fabled Silk Road city of Samarqand. Set in the aftermath of the death of Chaghadai, Chinggis Khan's second son whose line was regularly 'at odds' with their kinsman Qubilai (§52, p. 41), it is precipitated when the city's 'Saracens' demand that local Christian inhabitants return a great stone they had taken for the construction of a new church dedicated to John the Baptist. The Christians, 'very vexed', are at a loss over how to respond.

> Now a miracle occurred just as I will tell you: know that on the morning of the day when they were to return the stones, the column that was on the stone, through the will of our lord Jesus Christ, had removed itself from the stone to a height of three palms; and it was supported just as well as had been with the stone underneath it. From that day forward, this column has always remained, and is still, in that position. And it was and still is held to be one of the great miracles that has occurred in the world. (§52, p. 42)

Both dated to within living memory, the miracles of Baghdad and Samarqand take place in sites that had been ravaged by the Mongol conquests. Samarqand had been sacked during Chinggis Khan's sweep through Central Asia in 1220; in his *History of the World Conqueror*, the Persian historian Juvaini vividly described the destruction of its population.⁹ Baghdad, as already noted, was conquered by Qubilai's brother Hülegü in 1258. An Arabic *qasīda* (ode) penned by a scribe in the chancery of the Ayyubid rulers of Egypt and Syria (therefore presumably not an eyewitness to the events) laments that 'The Crown of the caliphate and the house whereby the rites of the Faith were exalted is laid waste by desolation.'¹⁰ Historical evidence suggests that the destruction of Baghdad was less dire than suggested in this poem, which recognizably belongs to the traditional Arabic genre of the city lament (*rithā' al-mudun*). It is as if the quick cut to tales of miracles – in the case of Samarqand, one that 'was and still is held to be one of the great miracles that has occurred in the world' (§52, p. 42) – is calculated to divert attention away from the Mongols' carefully cultivated reputation for wreaking devastation on all those who resisted them.

The Book of India

Where Marco clearly casts Qubilai and the Mongols as the greatest wonder of the world, Rustichello repeatedly touts the marvels of India as the heart of their book. After having described 'the people, animals, birds, gold, silver, stones, pearls, merchandise, and many other things of Mangi, Cathay, and many other provinces', Rustichello teases that their book is still

> missing all the facts about the Indians, which should be made known to those who do not know them, for there are many marvelous things that are nowhere else, for which it is very good and profitable to put them in writing in our book – and the master will set it down clearly, just as Messer Marco Polo tells and describes . . . And it is quite true that there are such marvelous things that the people who hear them will be amazed; nevertheless, we

will set them down in writing one after the other, just as
Messer Marco truthfully related them. (§157, p. 142)

India was a special site of marvels in both the Latin Christian
and Arabo-Islamic traditions. In Western sources it was a hazy,
mysterious land, home to the so-called 'monstrous races' inher-
ited from the first-century CE naturalist Pliny and other ancient
authors. In his *Book of the Treasure*, for example, the Florentine
Brunetto Latini writes in his entry on 'The Portion of the Orient
called Asia':

> You should know that in India . . . there are many different
> types of people . . . There are . . . people whose heads are
> those of dogs, and others whose eyes are in their shoulders
> because they have no heads. There are other people whose
> hair becomes white and hoary as soon as they are born,
> and in old age it turns black. Others have only one eye,
> and still others only one leg, and there are women who
> carry their children for five years but they do not live
> beyond the age of eight.[11]

For an educated thirteenth-century reader, such an account,
drawn from ancient Latin sources, would have carried the weight
of an authority lacking in Marco's *Description* – the hearsay of
a Venetian merchant. So automatic was the association of India
with such 'monstrous races' that in the early fifteenth century
John of Berry's *Book of Marvels* famously included the illustration of a blemmy (headless man) and a sciopod (one-legged man
whose giant foot served as a sunshade), neither of which are
mentioned in the text (illus. 38).

Turning to the Arabic tradition, *The Book of the Wonders of
India* (*Kitāb ajaib al-hind*), a late-ninth-/early tenth-century work
attributed to a Captain (*nakhuda*) Buzurg ibn Shahriyar of

38 Blemmyae, miniature from Marco Polo, *Le Livre des merveilles*,
1400–1420.

Ramhormuz, is a mix of 136 anecdotes from around the Indian
Ocean, collected orally from sources named and unnamed.
These various wonders include entries on land and sea creatures
(several each on whales, snakes, monkeys, giraffes, crocodiles),
human–animal hybrids, curiosities (like the Chinese garden
with flowers made of silk), and of the survivors or victims of
hazardous sea voyages.[12] Some closely anticipate marvels found
in the *Description*, like the male inhabitants of an island between
Fansur and Lamuri (Marco Polo's Lambri) who have tails.[13]

The most striking example of the intersection between different textual traditions is found in accounts of the Andamans,
an island group in the Bay of Bengal (between the Malay Peninsula
and the Indian subcontinent). The people here, Marco writes,
are 'well worth telling about' (§172, p. 155).

> Now know in all truth that all the men of this island have
> heads like dogs and teeth and eyes like dogs: for I tell you
> that they are all like the heads of great mastiffs. They have
> a lot of spices; they are a very cruel people; they eat as

many men as they can catch, if they are not their people. They have all kinds of spices in abundance; their food is rice, milk, and meat of all kinds; they also have fruit which is different from ours. (§172, p. 155)

Now, this mention of men with 'heads like dogs' is the one moment in the *Description* where Marco comes closest to Pliny's 'monstrous races' – in this case the cynocephali, here described as cannibals to boot. Yet nowhere in this passage does Marco flag this as a 'marvel', and indeed, it is remarkable how easily this account of animal-headed cannibals is interwoven with mundane features of commodities ('they have all kinds of spices in abundance') and foodways ('rice, milk, and meat of all kinds'). Having dutifully recorded these details, Marco is ready to move on to the more noteworthy island of Ceylon (Marco Polo's Sarandib).

Thus circumscribed, Chapter 172 seems to function as a repository for all Latin Europe's most reprehensible tropes about an abject other, predecessor to the most virulent kind of colonial discourse. Surprisingly, however, this account turns out to be part of a widespread textual tradition. Recognizable variants can be found in three works that precede the *Description*. The earliest, from the mid-ninth century, is the first part of *Accounts of China and India* (*Akhbār al-Sīn wa-l-Hind*), an Arabic text in two parts begun by an anonymous author from the Persian Gulf port of Siraf (and completed in the tenth century by Abū Zayd al-Sīrāfī); the second, *The Book of Curiosities of the Sciences and Marvels for the Eyes* (*Kitāb Gharā 'ib al funūn wa-mulah al-'uyūn*), an Arabic cosmological treatise composed in eleventh-century Egypt; and the third, the late twelfth-century *Description of Barbarous Peoples*, by the inspector of maritime trade in the Southern Song port of Quanzhou (Marco Polo's Zaytun). All three describe the islanders as black, with the first being particularly racialized and sexualized;

none calls them dog-headed, though the second notes that they 'devour human beings like dogs'. All three concur that they eat people alive, 'so that', as the final text puts it, 'sailors dare not anchor on this coast.'[4] Taken together with the *Description*, these variations on a theme offer a rare glimpse at the interconnected textual world based in the maritime trade routes of the premodern Indian Ocean system.

Elsewhere, Marco's 'Book of India' presents an assortment of marvels. His account of the Mongols' failed invasion of Japan features a mention of enchanted stones that protect their bearer from being harmed by iron. In the kingdom of Fansur (on the island of present-day Sumatra), Marco – in one of his rare evocations of first-hand experience – underscores the marvel of wheat (*farine*) made from trees: 'They make a lot of edible paste that is good to eat, for I tell you that we tried a lot of it ourselves, for we ate it several times' (§170, pp. 154–5). More frequently, his *merveilles* concern local customs and practices: Marco reports with equanimity that the king of Maabar goes around naked, even as the sheer quantity of 'beautiful pearls and other stones' with which he is bedecked is 'a marvel to see' (§174, p. 158). When that same king dies, the retainers that accompany him everywhere 'throw themselves in the fire and burn with the king to keep him company in the other world' (§174, p. 158). In his chapter on 'the Province of Lar', also on the east coast of India, Marco describes the asceticism of the 'Yogi', whom he defines as the 'regular clergy' (a phrase that aligns them with members of Latin Christian monastic orders) of the brahmins, who are 'the best merchants in the world and the most truthful' (§177, p. 165). These latter already lead temperate lives, avoiding meat, wine and lustful behaviour 'except with their wives' (p. 166). The Yogis, however, take this abstemiousness to a marvellous extreme, killing no animals, eating nothing green unless it is dried, sleeping on the ground completely naked with nothing over or under them: 'It's a great marvel that they don't die and that they live as long as I've described above. They are very abstemious in their food, for they fast all year and drink nothing other than water' (§177, p. 168). Far from the condemnation we might expect from the pen of a Latin Christian observer, we instead find praise at the honesty of the merchants and admiration for the asceticism of their 'regular clergy'.

Among the greatest wonders Marco encounters in his navigation of the Indian Ocean world are its geographical and climatological conditions. On the island of Lesser Java (Sumatra), he says: 'First I'll tell you something that everyone will take as a marvel. Know in truth that this island is so far south that the North Star does not appear in the slightest' (§166, p. 151). In the following chapter, he elaborates: 'what's more, I tell you the Master constellation [Ursa Major] doesn't appear at all' (§167, p. 152). Only at the southern tip of the Indian subcontinent does Marco reach a place from which 'you can see something of the North Star, which we have not seen from the island of Java until here. From this place, one went a good 30 miles out to sea and saw the North Star rising over the water by about a cubit' (§181, p. 173). Sailing up the Malabar coast, 'the North Star is higher; it seems to be about 2 cubits above the water' (§183, p. 174). Finally, reaching the kingdom of Gujarat, 'the polestar is even more pronounced, seeming a good six cubits high' (§184, p. 175). Marco's careful tracking of the reappearance and relative height of the North Star is a reminder of how disorienting the skies of the southern hemisphere would have seemed to the seafaring Venetians. Where the customs of brahmins and yogis can be assimilated to familiar Western types and even anthropophagy is registered only in passing, some of the most astonishing differences are to be found not among men but in the heavens.

FOUR

Animal, Vegetable, Mineral: Merchants and Their World

Information follows the same routes as ships and long-distance caravans . . . Information circulates, furthermore, with merchants, individuals who are generally inclined to remain discreet about supply points, modes of transaction, precise itineraries, and personal contacts, and who, when they prove talkative, are more often than not interested only in places of commerce and powers likely to favor their business.

FRANÇOIS-XAVIER FAUVELLE, *The Golden Rhinoceros: Histories of the African Middle Ages*[1]

In his crusade treatise *How to Defeat the Saracens* (c. 1314–18), the Dominican friar William of Adam identified India as 'truly and effectively, and not casually or occasionally', the cause of 'all the evils' besetting Latin Christendom's war effort against the Mamluks of Egypt. The reason?

For all of the things that are sold in Egypt, such as pepper, ginger, and other spices, gold and precious stones; silk and those precious materials dyed with the colors of India; and all other precious things are carried from India to Egypt. The merchants of these parts expose themselves to the fetters of xcommunication and put aside their obedience to the mother church and reverence

for the highest apostle when they go to Alexandria to
buy these things.[2]

William's condemnation reminds us that Latin Europe's appetite for the luxury goods of the East was fed by merchants like
the Venetians and the Genoese who obtained them from the
great ports of the eastern Mediterranean. Alexandria had long
been a primary centre for such trade; however, in 1291 – the
year in which the Polos set out for home – its importance suddenly intensified when the Mamluk sultan of Egypt conquered
Acre (as mentioned in the *Description* §194), the last crusader
outpost in the Middle East that had served as a terminus for
overland routes coming from the Persian Gulf or across Asia.
Reacting to ongoing hostilities with the Mamluks both preceding and following the fall of Acre, the pope had imposed
sanctions on any Latin Christians doing business in Egypt. This
prohibition threatened the business of Venetian, Genoese and
other Western merchants so seriously that they came more and
more surreptitiously to ignore them.

William of Adam's condemnation of commerce with the
Mamluks thus underscores the discrepancy between clerical and
commercial mentalities. Where a Dominican like William
divides the world into Christians versus 'Saracens', Marco Polo
sometimes seems to distinguish between merchants and everyone else in a way that cuts across religious difference. In the
kingdom of Dali (modern Yunnan province in southwest China),
Marco notes that there are 'many merchants and craftsmen
. . . the people are of several kinds; for there are people who
worship Muhammad, idolators, and a few Christians who are
Nestorians' (§118, p. 104). Nowhere is this world view more in
evidence than in his account of Baghdad, centre of the Islamic
world:

Baghdad is a very great city where the caliph of all the
world's Saracens is, just as the head of all the Christians
of the world is in Rome. Through the city flows a very
large river, and on this river one can well reach the
Indian Sea. There merchants come and go with their
merchandise. Know that, from Baghdad to the Indian
Sea, the river is a good 18 days' journey long; merchants
who wish to go to India follow this river down to a
city called Kish and from there enter the Indian Sea.
(§25, p. 20)

The same chapter also highlights the 1258 conquest of the city
by Qubilai's younger brother Hülegu, a world-historical event
that put an end to five hundred years of Abbasid rule. Marco –
or more likely, Rustichello – stages a dialogue between the
conqueror and the defeated caliph; eschewing any overt Latin
Christian moralizing, Hülegü condemns the latter's foolishness
in hoarding his wealth rather than using it to hire mercenaries
to defend his realm. Meanwhile, Marco focuses on the comings
and goings of merchants engaged in the India trade – the majority of whom would certainly have been Muslim – shuttling back
and forth between Baghdad and the Persian Gulf.

William of Adam's scathing denunciation of merchants trading for spices and other luxuries from the Indies in Alexandria
reminds us that, between fifteen and twenty years after Marco
and Rustichello completed their *Description*, Egypt remained
the point of access for such commodities in the eyes of most
Latin Christians. In this light, in what to us reads as a repetitive
and formulaic listing of the goods to be found in this city or
that province, their contemporaries would undoubtedly have
been riveted by the information and eager to learn the sources
of the precious goods they normally acquired in ports such as
Alexandria through the intermediary of non-Christian merchants.

In the mid-tenth-century *Accounts of China and India*, Abū Zayd
al-Sirāfī described the riches of

> the Sea of India and China, in whose depths are pearls and
> ambergris, in whose rocky isles are gems and mines of gold,
> in the mouths of whose beasts is ivory, in whose forests
> grow ebony, sapan wood, rattans, and trees that bear
> aloewood, camphor, nutmeg, cloves, sandalwood, and
> all manner of fragrant and aromatic spices, whose birds
> are *fafaghā* (parrots, that is) and peacocks, and the
> creeping things of those earth are civet cats and musk
> gazelles, and all the rest that no one could enumerate,
> so many are its blessings.[3]

What were these exotic commodities – animal, vegetable and
mineral – that merchants trafficked across Eurasia? How were
they used in different parts of the premodern world? And what
does Marco Polo have to tell us about their sources?

Animal

Animals were central to life in the premodern world in ways
practically unimaginable today. Sheep, goats, cattle, camels and,
of course, horses were fundamental, especially to nomadic pastor-
alists like the Mongols and other Central Asian peoples. Rulers
in South and Southeast Asia deployed elephants in battle and
rode them in ceremonial performances of kingship. As we saw
in the last chapter, Marco Polo delights in animals throughout
the *Description*. The same narrator who dispassionately describes
customs like human cremation, which would have been shock-
ing to his Christian audience, reserves some his most expressive
language for accounts of the fauna found in various regions of
the world. His enthusiasm is often linked to the leitmotif of

diversity, emphasized from the opening lines of the text. Throughout, cultural difference is domesticated through comparison to familiar Latin European examples – like the Nestorian Catholicos of Baghdad (head of the Church of the East) who conducts business 'just like the pope of Rome' (§24, p. 19) or the Indian 'yogis' whom Marco calls 'regular clergy' (§177, p. 167), evoking Western monks who live by the 'rules' of their order. Mentions of animals and birds, on the other hand, emphasize their novelty, as in the case of the Coromandel coast of southeastern India, where the fauna are 'different from ours in diverse ways' (§174, p. 161). On the southwestern coast of India, Quilon has 'many diverse animals', including lions and peacocks, 'different from all others in the world . . . more beautiful and better . . . on account of the great heat there' (§180, p. 172). Most memorably, Badakhshan, the mountainous region in the northeastern part of modern Afghanistan, boasts 'a multitude of very large wild sheep, with horns a good six palms . . . From these horns the shepherds make big bowls that they eat from. The shepherds also use these horns to enclose the spaces where they keep their

39 Marco Polo sheep (*Ovis ammon polii*).

animals' (§50, p. 40). Today, these magnificent animals – the focus of big-game hunters and conservationists alike – are known as Marco Polo sheep or, more formally, by the Latin name *Ovis ammon polii* (illus. 39).

For a merchant like Marco Polo, however, animals were crucially important as sources of several of the luxury commodities traded widely across the medieval world, as he is careful to note throughout the *Description*.

A World of Scents: Ambergris and Musk

Often synthetically produced today, authentic ambergris and musk were staples in medieval perfumery and *materia medica*. In his *Book of Ceremonies*, the tenth-century Byzantine emperor Constantine VII named both (together with sugar, frankincense and cinnamon) as supplies to be taken on military campaigns. From about the same time at the other end of the Mediterranean, an inscription on the lid of an ivory pyxis (cylindrical container) from Madinat al-Zahra, the caliphal palace-city at the heart of Muslim Spain, proclaims: 'I am a vessel for camphor and musk and ambergris' (illus. 40). Their value in medieval Islamic culture is attested by mentions in Arabic treatises such as Ibn Māsawaīh's *On Simple Aromatic Substances*, al-Kindi's ninth-century *Book of the Chemistry of Perfume* and poet al-Sarī bin Muhammad al-Raffā's tenth-century *Book of the Beloved and What Is Smelled and What Is Drunk*.

Though frequently paired, ambergris and musk came from quite different animal sources. Ambergris (Arabic *anbar*) is a waxy secretion from the digestive tract of sperm whales, generated – like pearls in an oyster – to surround irritants like cuttlefish quills. It was thus a maritime product. Harvested floating on the waters or cast up on the shores of the Indian Ocean, its sources long remained mysterious, variously postulated to be the upwelling from an underwater spring, a sea fungus or the dung of a sea creature. The anonymous continuator of *Accounts of China and India*, writing (in Arabic) from his vantage point in the Persian Gulf, reports that 'it is found in the form of "eggs", rounded and bluish gray'; on moonlit nights, specially trained camels 'scan the shore for ambergris, and when they spot some, they kneel so that their riders can dismount and pick it up'. At other times, he continues, ambergris can be found floating in the sea, where it is swallowed by whales; fishermen capture the whales and harvest the substance from their bellies.

> Any of the ambergris that has been in contact with
> the whale's stomach is *mand*, the sort with the rancid
> and fishy smell stocked by the druggists in Madinat
> al-Salām (Baghdad) and Basra; any ambergris uncon-
> taminated by the rancidness of the whale's stomach
> will be extremely pure.[4]

In the Latin West, the Old French *ambre gris* or grey amber (source of our modern English word 'ambergris') was set in rela-tion to *ambre jaune* or yellow amber, the fossilized tree resin often cast up on the shores of the Baltic Sea, since both were harvested from the water.

Ambergris, then, was sourced in the western part of the Indian Ocean system. *The Accounts of China and India* reports that the 'finest sort' came from 'Barbarā' (the Somali coast), the land of the Zanj (the east African coast south of the equator) and around the port of al-Shihr on the Arabian peninsula. Marco Polo, who likely learned about ambergris at second hand from Muslim trav-elling companions and fellow merchants plying the Indian Ocean trade, largely concurs, naming as its sources the 'island of Mogdasio' (likely Mogadishu on the Somali coast) and Zanzibar, 'because a lot of whales are taken there' (§192, p. 183). However, eschewing the *Account*'s more colourful claims, he simply reminds

40 Ivory pyxis, Madinat al-Zahra, c. 966.

his readers: 'you know that whales make ambergris' (§191, p. 181), omitting the fabulous tale of their swallowing free-floating 'eggs'.

Unknown in Greek and Roman antiquity, ambergris, with its sources in the western Indian Ocean, came to be highly prized in the medieval Islamic world. Its medicinal properties were praised by luminaries such as the Persian physician and polymath al-Rāzī in the tenth century, Ibn Sīnā (Avicenna) in the eleventh century and the Andalusian philosopher Ibn Rushd (Averroes) in the twelfth. Like musk, it was used as a fixative for perfumes. It appears in numerous concoctions in *Scents and Flavours the Banqueter Favours* (*Kitāb al-Wuslah ilāl-Habīb fi Wasf al-Tayyibāt wal Tīb*), a thirteenth-century Syrian work from the 'golden age' of Arabic cookbooks – especially in perfumes, which are generically called '*anbarīnā*. To make a 'sandalwood '*anbarīnā*, popular in summer and in hot weather to cool the humors': 'Scrape Maqasiri sandalwood with rose water, shape, and spread out in a china bowl. Smoke five times with ambergris, shape it with gum tragacanth dissolved with rose water and musk, and make into '*anbarīnā*. It is the best.'[5] Ambergris may be added to beverages or used to smoke the liquid or (most commonly) the vessel it is served in. It is also used in a breath-freshening tablet, a hand-washing powder, and in recipes for lamb and chicken dishes.

Like ambergris, musk, the glandular secretion of (in Marco Polo's words) 'a little animal as big as a gazelle' (§72, p. 61), was used in perfumery, medicine and cooking. In an ode by Unsurī, the court poet of Mahmūd of Ghazna (in today's eastern Afghanistan), the garden of the vizier's palace is adorned by a 'musk-perfumed spring'. In the cookbook *Scents and Flavours*, it is used in some of the same ways and even in some of the same recipes as ambergris; in addition, musk is used to finish pickles, in rice pilafs, and in a wide variety of sweets and baked goods – often in combination with rose water. Fakhraddin Gorgani's mid-eleventh-century Persian romance *Vis and Ramin* hints that it was more highly prized than ambergris: seeking to convince Vis of Ramin's superiority over all other suitors, her nurse opines: 'If they are stars, he is the sun; if they are ambergris, he is pure musk.'[6] In *The Ultimate Ambition in the Arts of Erudition*, an encyclopaedia compiled a decade or two after the *Description*, the Egyptian bureaucrat Shihīb al-Dīn al-Nuwayrī gave musk pride of place in his chapter on aromatics. He names Tibet as its source; citing previous authorities, he explains that differences in quality reflect the length of time the musk has spent in transit (Khorasan in eastern Iran being a favoured route) or the pasturage on which the animals it came from had grazed.

Becoming better known than ambergris in the Latin West, musk was especially important to the Polos. Among the possessions inventoried at Marco's death in 1324 were three boxes of musk worth 217 ducats. Previously, his uncle's will of 1310 showed Marco and Maffeo accepting musk in partial payment of a debt owed them by a business partner; that same year, Marco and his half-brother formed a temporary partnership (*collegantia*) with a fellow Venetian for the sale of 1½ pounds of musk – a deal that went bad when that travelling partner failed to return the full amount of the profit owed and left some of the musk unaccounted for. Meanwhile, musk served as part of the collateral Marco received for a loan made to the wife of a spice dealer. We do not know if the Polos' interest in musk pre-dated their travels through Asia but after their return to Venice it clearly became central to the business ventures of the entire family. Thus it is not surprising to see musk capturing Marco's attention throughout the *Description*. The 'best and the finest musk oxen in the world', he notes, come from the province of Tangut (the former kingdom of the Western Xia, in northwestern China). When these creatures are caught,

> a cyst of blood is found in its belly, between the skin and the flesh. You slice it, together with the skin, and draw it out. This blood is the musk which emits such a great odor. Know that in this country there's a great quantity of it and good, as I have told you. (§72, p. 61)

In Tibet, he writes, the animals that make musk are called *gudderi* (§115, p. 101); in Jiandu (modern Sichuan province), 'Hunters catch them and extract the musk in great quantity' (§117, p. 103).

Finally, 'animals that make musk' are included among the roe deer, fallow deer, black squirrels and gyrfalcons in the park within the outer walls of the Great Khan's palace in Khanbaliq (§84, p. 74) – presumably part of the bounty Qubilai commandeered from the lands under his rule to enhance the grandeur of his imperial capital.

While it is easy for us to imagine a Middle Ages permeated by unpleasant odours, the prominence that Marco accords ambergris and musk reminds us that it was also a highly perfumed world.

Pearls

Before their meteoric rise to power, the Mongols knew freshwater pearls that came from the rivers of northern Manchuria, their ancestral homeland. Their campaigns of conquest, however, soon gave them access to higher-quality saltwater pearls in astonishing quantities. The Persian historian Rashīd al-Dīn reports that when the Jin emperor of northern China submitted to Chinggis Khan in 1226, his tribute gifts included trays of magnificent round pearls. After distributing a pearl to all of his followers with pierced ears, he ordered the remainder scattered 'so that the people can gather them up'. Two generations later, under Qubilai, the Mongol court carefully controlled the circulation and redistribution of pearls. As we saw earlier, pearls were among the prized commodities (along with precious stones, gold, silver and silk) that merchants were regularly required to submit to the imperial treasury in exchange for paper money. At the Great Khan's New Year's celebration, the governors and tributary rulers of his subject provinces, regions and kingdoms brought offerings of pearls (again along with gold, silver, precious stones and rich white cloths) so that 'he be pleased and happy all year long' (§89, p. 79). The quantities fished from a lake in the province of Jiandu (present-day Sichuan province) were strictly regulated, lest overharvesting reduce their value:

'when the great lord wishes, he has some extracted for himself alone; but no one else can extract them without being killed' (§117, p. 103). Most pearls, however, came from India, reaching Khanbaliq via the recently conquered ports of southern China: Fuzhou, with its 'great market in pearls and other precious stones' (§156, p. 140), and especially Zaytun, where the 'many big, good-quality pearls', like other 'precious stones of great worth' were imported, were taxed at a rate of 10 per cent (§157, p. 141).

What became of this flood of pearls? Under Qubilai, pearls were ubiquitous in Mongol ceremonial dress. In Anige's famous portrait of Qubilai Khan's chief wife, Chabi (illus. 1), her *boqta* (the tall cylindrical headdress worn by Mongol women on courtly occasions) features pearls clustered in floral designs and in long intertwined strands hanging on either side of the khatun's head to several inches below her shoulders. Pearls 'very nobly' decorate the thirteen sets of *jisun* (robes of one colour) that the Great Khan distributes to the 12,000 members of his imperial guard on ceremonial occasions (§90, p. 80).

Given the importance of pearls to the Mongol economy and culture, it is no surprise that they appear frequently in Marco's text. In Japan, he says, the pearls are 'red, very beautiful, round, and fat', their worth 'equal to or greater than that of white ones' (§159, p. 144). But the greatest quantities, as we have seen, come from India. In Maabar, merchants formed companies that equipped a fleet of small boats. Once out at sea, brahmins 'enchant[ed]' the fish so they would not harm the divers, who:

> go underwater [and] stay under as long as they can. When they are at the bottom of the sea, they find there what men call sea oysters; and in this oyster are found pearls, big and little, of all kinds, for the pearls are found in their flesh. In this way pearls are fished, in such very grand quantities that it can't be told, for know that the

pearls that are found in this sea are spread throughout the whole world. (§174, pp. 157–8)

The king of this land wore a necklace of '104 very large and beautiful pearls and rubies of very great worth' strung on a silken cord (§174, p. 158) – part of the 'very great treasure' amassed from the 10 per cent levy placed on the harvest. Those without direct access to pearl fisheries had, according to Marco, to resort to other strategies, like the 'rich and very wealthy king' of Lar (an Indian province that scholars have not been able to identify), who:

> arranged with all the merchants in his land that all
> the pearls they bring him from the Maabar kingdom . . .
> where the best pearls are found, that he will pay them
> twice as much as they bought them for. And the brahmins
> go to the kingdom of Maabar and buy all the good pearls
> that they find and then bring them to their king, and tell
> him truthfully what they spent. The king immediately has
> them given twice what they spent, and they never get less.
> For this reason, they have brought him great quantities of
> very good and big ones. (§177, p. 166)

Pearls from Maabar, as we have seen, travelled via the maritime route to the great ports of southern China: as Marco says of Fuzhou, its market abounds in pearls and other precious stones 'because many ships from India come here with many merchants, who frequent the isles of India' (§156, p. 140).

But pearls spread westward as well, notably to Hormuz on the Persian Gulf, the transhipment point where merchants brought pearls, 'all kinds of spices, precious stones, . . . cloths of silk and gold, elephant tusks, and much other merchandise' from India to 'sell . . . to other men who then transport them

all over the world, selling them to other people' (§37, p. 30).
This, as we know, was one route by which such Indian luxuries
reached the port of Alexandria, there to be trafficked to Venetian
and Genoese middlemen. But the journey could be eventful. To
reach Hormuz, ships had to navigate the dangerous waters off
the coast of Gujarat, where pearls were among the booty sought
by pirates:

> In this kingdom [are] the most corsairs in the world,
> and I tell you that they commit such bad deeds as I will
> describe. For know that when these bad corsairs capture
> merchants, they make them drink tamarind and seawater
> so that the merchants get sick and throw up everything
> in their stomachs. The corsairs gather everything the
> merchants throw up and search through it to see if there
> are pearls or other precious stones, for the corsairs say that
> when merchants are taken, they eat the pearls and other
> precious stones so that the corsairs won't find them.
> (§184, p. 175)

Predictably, Marco condemns as 'bad' those people and practices
that harm merchants, with no mention of their religion, ethnicity or political allegiance. Those fortunate enough to make it past
these Gujarati pirates and other maritime hazards could then
continue on to Hormuz, in the Persian Gulf, and Aden, at the
southwestern tip of the Arabian peninsula guarding the entrance
to the Red Sea, 'where all the ships from India come with all their
merchandise' (§194, p. 187), from there to be transported
onward to Alexandria.

Horses

In economic histories of the Middle Ages, it is a truism that the
appetite for spices, pearls and other luxuries from India and

Southeast Asia created a West-to-East drain of precious metals, especially silver, which would have significant consequences in world history. While this was certainly true for Latin Europe, parts of the Islamic world – notably Persia and the Arabian peninsula – benefited from a commodity of their own that could be exchanged for the goods coming to ports like Hormuz and Aden: horses. Interestingly, the *Description* allows us to connect some of the dots of a long-distance intra-Asian trade all but invisible to historians of the medieval West. For example, the Ilkhanate – Mongol Persia, ruled by the descendants of Qubilai's brother Hülegü – boasts:

> many fine warhorses, many of which are taken to India to be sold. Know that they are very valuable horses, for each one sells for a good 200 pounds *tournois*, and most of them are that valuable . . . The people of this kingdom take the horses that I've mentioned to Qays and Hormuz, which are two cities on the banks of the Indian Sea. There they find merchants who buy them and take them to India and sell them there for the high prices I have told you. (§33, p. 27)

What fuels this export trade? In his account of the Coromandel (southeastern) coast of India, Marco explains:

> I . . . tell you that no horses are born in this kingdom; therefore, all the treasure from the yield they have each year, or most of it, is used to buy horses. I will tell you how. Know in all truth merchants from Hormuz, Kish, Dhofar, al-Shihr, and Aden – these provinces have many . . . warhorses and other horses – merchants from these provinces, as I have told you, buy good horses and load them in ships and bring them to this king, and also to his brothers, who are 4 other kings; they sell them each for a

good 500 gold *saggi*, which are worth more than 100 silver
marks. I tell you that this king buys a good 2,000 each
year, and his brothers buy as many, and by the end of the
year not one of them has 100: all of them die, because they
have no marshals, nor do they know how to care for them,
but they die for ill care. I also tell you that the merchants
who bring these horses to sell do not permit or take any
marshals with them, for they want the horses to die on
these kings. (§174, p. 159)

Ships 'laden with merchandise and horse' from the southern
Arabian peninsula and the Persian Gulf sailed to the port of
Qa'il. Ruled by the eldest of the five brothers, it was 'a good
place and market for trading' since 'many merchants from many
parts [came] to buy merchandise, horses, and other things' (§179,
p. 171). While both Latin Europe and the Islamic world faced
trade deficits fuelled by their import of goods from South and
Southeast Asia, Marco Polo lifts the curtain on the way the latter
helped balance the books through this lesser-known aspect of
the premodern Indian Ocean system.

Vegetable

To measure the long-lasting impact of the medieval spice trade,
take a bottle of pumpkin pie spice off the shelf and scan its
contents. Of its most common ingredients, only allspice (so
named because it is thought to combine the taste of the others)
comes from the New World; the rest – cinnamon, ginger, cloves
and nutmeg – all originate in South or Southeast Asia and, in
Marco Polo's day, would have reached Europe through the
overland or (more likely) maritime trade routes we have been
exploring. William of Adam, as we have seen, railed against the
India trade for the way it attracted Latin Christian, especially

Italian, merchants to do business in the Mamluk-ruled port of
Alexandria. Yet just five years or so before he penned his screed,
another author, writing (like Marco and Rustichello) in French,
gave this account of the goods flowing into the markets of
Alexandria:

> Before the great river enters Egypt, people who are used
> to doing so cast their fishing nets wide across the river
> each evening. When morning comes they find in the nets
> such goods as are sold by weight when imported into this
> country, by which I mean ginger, rhubarb, aloewood, and
> cinnamon. It is said that these things come from the
> earthly paradise, that the wind brings them down from
> the trees in paradise just as in this country the wind brings
> down the dry wood in the forests.[7]

The text is *The Life of Saint Louis* (1309), a hagiographic biography of the French king Louis IX (d. 1270, canonized 1297),
whose author, Jean de Joinville, was the late king's subject and
loyal companion. This description of the Nile sets the stage for
his account of the crusader-king's disastrous Egyptian campaign
of 1249–50. It unfolds on two levels: the 'factual' account of Eastern spices fished from the river, which gives way to the second-
hand explanation ('it is said') of their ultimate source in the
earthly Paradise (evoking the four 'rivers of Paradise' of Genesis
2:10–14).

Jean de Joinville's direct experience of Egypt was nearly half
a century old by the time the *Description* was composed. Nevertheless, the fact that such an account could still be written in
the first decade of the fourteenth century illustrates the dispar-
ity of perspectives on the India trade even among people living
in close geographical or cultural proximity. For William the crusade apologist, the Western pursuit of Eastern luxuries was to be

condemned because of the way it enticed Christian merchants to do business with, and thus to profit, the Mamluk sultans of Egypt. For Jean, a veteran of the French king's mid-thirteenth-century crusade against the Mamluks' predecessors the Ayyubids (descendants of the celebrated Muslim ruler Saladin), exotic goods from the East were flotsam harvested from the Nile, originating in one of the four rivers of Paradise. In this light, Marco Polo's enumeration of the 'great abundance' of pepper, ginger, cinnamon and other spices grown in the 'kingdom of Malabar' (§183, p. 174) or the 'pepper, nutmeg, spikenard, galangal, cubeb, cloves, and all the expensive spices you can find in the world' to be had on 'the great island of Java' (§163, p. 149), far from a routine or even tedious inventory, would have struck his contemporaries as a tantalizing revelation of the ultimate source of the valued commodities they were accustomed to acquire from Muslim intermediaries in the port of Alexandria. Even more remarkable were the details he supplies on sites in East Asia, as in his description of the inland city of Suzhou (modern Jiuquan, in Gansu province): 'I . . . tell you that in the mountains of this city, rhubarb and ginger grow in great abundance; for I tell you that for a Venetian groat you could get a good 40 pounds of fresh ginger, which is very good' (§151, p. 132).

But the main products driving the spice trade came from the maritime routes to South and Southeast Asia. In this section we explore two of those commodities, pepper and camphor, and some of their uses in the medieval world.

Pepper

The kingdom of Malabar (modern Kerala on the southwest Indian coast), Marco Polo writes, has 'a great abundance of pepper, and ginger, too. There is also a lot of cinnamon, and there is also a great quantity of other spices, turpeth, and Indian nuts' (§183, p. 174). Although mentioned here only fleetingly, black pepper (*Piper nigrum*) is in fact native to this region, which remained its primary producer through the sixteenth century. Peppercorns were grown in the interior uplands, then trafficked by middlemen to Muslim merchants in coastal settlements like Quilon (modern Kollam), Hili and Gujarat; from there, they were shipped by sea both westward to the Islamic world and eastward to China. As Marco Polo reminds us, 'for each ship-load of pepper going to Alexandria or other places to be carried to Christian lands, a hundred [shiploads] come to this port of Zaytun,' where it is the source of great revenue, since the levy on pepper is 44 per cent (§157, p. 141).

Famously, pepper was central to the spice trade to the medieval West, where it had been popular since Roman times. Of all the recipes in the first-century CE cookbook attributed to Apicius, 80 per cent of them called for substantial amounts – an extravagance that both confounded and irritated the irascible naturalist Pliny the Elder, who found it disagreeable in taste and appearance: 'To think that its only pleasing quality is bitterness and that we go all the way to India to get this!', he complained.[8] In medieval Galenic medicine, according to which health represented an equilibrium of the four 'humours', pepper, like most spices, was considered 'hot' and 'dry', so valuable in balancing out 'cold' foods (including meats like beef, goose, crane, brains and tongue) as well as 'moist' ones (like most raw fruits and vegetables). Although expensive, it was still affordable enough to be relatively widespread. In the First Crusade, Genoese infantrymen who took part in the conquest of Caesaria in 1100 were each awarded 45 silver solidi and two pounds of peppercorns. A mid-thirteenth-century satirical verse by the French poet Rutebeuf shows sellers of 'pepper and cumin' scorned by a herbalist who claims to have been the doctor of the 'Lord of Cairo'. And an anonymous poem from the turn of the fourteenth century, roughly contemporary with the *Description*, features a mercer hawking all manner of clothing and accessories who also trafficks in pepper, cumin and other exotic spices like ginger, galangal and saffron.

In our thirteenth-century Syrian cookbook *Scents and Flavours*, pepper – absent from the kinds of aromatic compounds in which musk or ambergris are featured – seasons a wide assortment of prepared foods: chicken, aubergine (eggplant) and especially lamb dishes; these include a Georgian kebab which, the author writes, 'I once made for my uncle al-Malik al-Ashraf, may God the exalted shower him with mercy' (§6.14, p. 81) and *narjisiyyah*, a stew topped with eggs (the yolk and white evoking a narcissus flower). Pepper is also used to season breadcrumb stuffings, numerous cold and picked dishes, a rich egg bread associated with 'Franks and Armenians' (§7.103, p 191) and appears in a cure for nausea! Today paired with salt – a mineral essential to life and an important driver of trade throughout human history – pepper has a long storied past as the quintessential imported luxury.

Camphor

In his 'Book of India', Marco Polo reports that the kingdom of Fansur produces 'the best camphor in the world' that 'sells for its weight in gold' (§170, p. 154). Obtained from trees, it was, as the encyclopaedist al-Nuwayrī writes, 'the most noble of all resins and the most entitled to be placed first in the list because of its prevalence in various types of compound medicines and fragrances'.[9] At the eighth-century Tang court in China, a fine grade received in tribute from today's northern Vietnam was moulded into cicada- and silkworm-shaped amulets to be worn in the folds of one's clothing. In *Scents and Flavours*, it appears in perfumed distillations – especially paired with rose water, as in a camphor water blend that 'surpasses every perfume'.[10] Al-Nuwayrī, for his part, expounds on its medicinal uses by quoting the great eleventh-century Persian physician Avicenna (Ibn Sina):

> Camphor is cold and dry in the third degree, and using it quickens the advent of gray hair. It prevents hot swellings and when mixed with vinegar or the juice of unripe dates, myrtle water, or sweet basil water, it prevents nosebleeds. It helps to heal burning headaches and strengthens the senses of the feverish. It diminishes sexual desire and creates kidney and bladder stones.[11]

Camphor also appears in cooking. In *Scents and Flavours*, it is used like musk and ambergris, and often in combination with them. It appears in the title of 'Camphor white meatballs', a minced chicken and lamb dish that calls for Chinese cinnamon, coriander seeds, ginger, cumin and other ingredients including nuts and rose water. Camphor appears nowhere in the dish but is meant to signal its colour: one pounds the combined meats with a cleaver 'to the consistency of peppercorns', turning the mixture white.[12] So familiar had camphor become that it, like pepper, featured not just as an ingredient but as a metaphor to guide the cook and, perhaps, to whet the appetite of the potential diner.

Marco Polo's identification of the source of the most desirable camphor conforms to received opinion spanning the Old World from the Mediterranean to the Pacific. The *Accounts of China and India*, reflecting the experience of mid-ninth-century Arabo-Persian merchants from the Persian Gulf, likewise lists the island kingdom of Fansur as the source of the highest grade of camphor. The twelfth-century *Description of Barbarous Peoples* concurs, adding that it comes from a pine-like tree that grows 'in the depths of the hills and the remotest valleys'.[13] Harvesters fell the trees and notch the wood; the camphor oozes out and forms crystals. On the shores of the Mediterranean, our ency-clopaedist al-Nuwayrī confirms that the camphor of Fansur is 'the finest of all types', whereas 'the worst kind' comes from al-Zābaj (nearby Java). This convergence of opinion concerning Fansur strikingly illustrates the way the *Description*, though com-posed in French in late thirteenth-century Genoa, is embedded in a network of mercantile knowledge spanning many centuries in several languages, reaching from Zaytun on the straits of Taiwan to the Mediterranean.

Interestingly, however, Marco makes no mention of the per-fumery, medicinal or culinary uses of camphor common across Islamic West Asia. Rather, he recounts its role in embalming and funerary practices in South and East Asia. In Tangut (the Tibeto-Burman kingdom of Xi Xia, conquered by the Mongols in 1227), the bodies of the dead are placed in a casket, covered with cloths and, he says, 'arrange[d] with camphor and other spices so that the body's stink doesn't affect those in the house' (§58, p. 46). The *Accounts of China and India* gives a similar report about the Chinese: that bodies are covered in quicklime and that their ruler is embalmed in aloes and camphor – purchased at twice the market price, thus artificially inflating prices (§1.8.3–5, p. 17). In Ceylon (Marco Polo's Sarandib), camphor is used together with sandalwood and saffron in royal funeral pyres (§1.9.2, p. 24). Finally, in contrast to its use for the burial or cremation of kings, Marco describes how the people in one of the kingdoms on the island of Sumatra take small monkeys 'whose faces are like men's', remove all their hair except on their chins and chests, then 'dry them and shape them and rub them with camphor and other things so that they seem to have been human'. This, Marco asserts with uncharacteristic indignation, is 'a great lie and deception' (§166, p. 152).

Minerals

Gems

In the chapter 'Qualities of Places with Respect to Different Things' in *The Ultimate Ambition*, the encyclopedist al-Nuwayrī writes: 'With jewels, one talks of the turquoise of Nishapur, the rubies of Sarandīb, the pearls of Oman, the emeralds of Egypt, the carnelian of Yemen, the onyx of Zafār, the garnets of Balkh, and the coral of Ifrīqiya.'[4] The *Description*, of course, is organized not according to material objects (in this case, precious stones) but by geography. Still, mapping the convergences and divergences between these two roughly contemporary accounts provides a fascinating picture of the knowledge available to the bookish bureaucrat working largely from authoritative writings in the Arabic tradition on the one hand, and the Venetian merchant in the service of the Great Khan, combining his own eyewitness experience with hearsay testimony, on the other. Pearls, as we have seen, recur frequently throughout the work, both for their privileged place in Mongol court ceremonials and for the details concerning their harvesting and circulation. The other gems mentioned by al-Nuwayrī occur more sporadically – the discrepancies affording more insight into Marco Polo's relation to the pan-Asian traffic in both goods and knowledge.

Turquoise provides an interesting case in point. For al-Nuwayrī, writing to establish the 'Qualities of Places with Respect to Different Things', they are associated with the fabled Silk Road city of Nishapur. Founded by the pre-Islamic Sasanian king Shapur I in the third century CE, it went on to serve as the capital of several subsequent Muslim empires centred in Greater Khorasan (today's northeastern Iran and western Afghanistan). Occurring exclusively in desert regions, this 'sky blue stone' would come to symbolize imperial splendour across early modern Islamic Eurasia. Ottoman, Safavid and Mughal sultans and emperors exchanged turquoise as gifts and featured its colour prominently in their architecture and material culture – a visibility that perhaps helps account for the interest that European traders began to show in the stone in the sixteenth century. Marco Polo, for his part, calls them 'very beautiful stones' (§117, p. 103), situating them not in Khorasan (which figures little in the *Description*) but in the Persian kingdom of Kerman (in southeastern Iran). Notably, he also names a Chinese source: Jiandu, where the Great Khan exercises a monopoly on its extraction.

Several of al-Nuwayrī's other stones garner little to no mention in the *Description*. Carnelian and onyx are absent altogether. Emeralds appear only among the other precious gems in the strings worn by the king of Maabar. Coral is an interesting case. As al-Nuwayrī notes, it comes from Ifrīqiya (the kingdom or province around modern-day Tunisia), or more precisely, the Mediterranean waters between Tunisia and Sicily. It was one of few Western luxury goods that could be marketed in Asia: as Marco writes of Kashmir, 'coral taken *from our land* to sell is sold in this country more than any others' (§49, p. 40, emphasis added).

Quite the opposite is true of rubies: the *Description*'s chapter on Ceylon exactly mirrors al-Nuwayrī's attribution of rubies to the island of Sarandib. Marco calls them 'the most precious thing in the world': 'I tell you that on this island, good and noble rubies grow that grow nowhere else in the world' (§173, p. 156).

Ceylon, as we recall, is the site of a great mountain taken to be the sacred burial place of Sakyamuni Buddha by Buddhists, and of 'Adam our first father' by Muslims. Buzurg ibn Shahriyar's *Book of the Wonders of India*, a freewheeling late ninth-/early tenth-century source from the Persian Gulf, brings the two together, describing the site where Adam's footprint is to be found as 'a mountain of rubies and diamonds that is hard to climb'.[15] (Our other ninth-/tenth-century Persian Gulf text, the *Accounts of China and India*, makes no mention of rubies or any other gemstones.) Marco Polo's version, however, adds a contemporary twist:

> The king of this province has the most beautiful ruby that was ever seen or that can be seen in the whole world[:] it is about a palm long and every bit as thick as a man's arm; it is the most splendid thing in the world to see; it is free of flaws; it is red as fire; it is of such great worth that it could hardly be bought for money. (§173, p. 156)

Earlier, we saw Qubilai Khan requisitioning objects taken to be relics of the Buddha for himself. Here again, he is quick to demand another one of Ceylon's unique treasures: 'I tell you in truth that the Great Khan sent his messenger to this king and said that he wanted to buy this ruby and that, if he would give it to him, he would give him the worth of a city' (§173, p. 156). This time, however, Qubilai's desire is thwarted: 'This king said that he would not give it for anything in the world, for he said that it belonged to his ancestors; and for this reason he could not have it for anything in the world' (§173, p. 156). His refusal is all the more striking since the men of the island 'are not men-at-arms'. This one-of-a-kind ruby unexpectedly reveals the limits of the Great Khan's tributary power.

At the same time, Marco describes two stones not mentioned in al-Nuwayrī's *Ultimate Ambition*. First there are diamonds, which come, he says, from 'nowhere in the whole world' but Motupalli, the thirteenth-century kingdom of the Kakatiyas on the east coast of India, where they are found 'in great quantity'. The local people harvest them, he relates, in three ways. First, stones dislodged when torrential rains rush through the great mountain gorges are collected when the water recedes. Second, men extract the stones from rocky caverns, braving large poisonous snakes and the blistering summer heat. Third, and most fantastically: men toss pieces of meat into the deep and inaccessible mountain valleys. The diamonds stick to the meat. Then white eagles attracted to the valley by the snakes living there carry off the diamond-studded pieces of meat. Hunters track the birds and either scare them off and extract the diamonds from the meat left behind or, if the birds have already eaten it, the hunters wait to collect 'plenty more diamonds' from the eagles' dung. Perhaps counterintuitively, it is precisely where Marco's report sounds the most fanciful that it turns out to dovetail with more widespread, often orally circulated Asian traditions. In his *Book of the Wonders of India*, Buzurg ibn Shahriyar tells a nearly identical tale set not in Ceylon but in Kashmir and using vultures rather than eagles. Yet another similar account comes from an Eastern Christian source in the fourth-century Mediterranean; in his lapidary (a treatise on gems), the Cypriot bishop Epiphanius of Salamis writes that, among precious stones mentioned in the Bible, jacinths are retrieved by tossing meat into the 'Scythian gorges' where they are found.[16] As for the bounty of Ceylon: 'Do not think that the good diamonds come to our Christian lands,' Marco (or perhaps Rustichello) cautions; rather, 'they go and are carried to the Great Khan and to the kings and barons of varied regions and kingdoms, for they have great treasure and buy all the expensive stones' (§175, p. 163).

In the *Description*, Marco Polo devotes a long passage on the kingdom of Badakhshan (northeastern Afghanistan and eastern Tajikistan) to its mineral wealth. Pride of place goes to 'the precious stones called *balasci*, very beautiful and of great worth, that come from rocks in the mountains'. These are balas rubies or spinels – perhaps the garnets that al-Nuwayrī links to the fabled Silk Road city of Balkh, some 500 kilometres (310 mi.) to the west, sacked by the Mongols in circa 1220. Mining them, from 'great [manmade] caverns in the mountains [that] go very deep', just like silver mines, is a royal monopoly: to extract or export them without permission is a capital offence. Like the rubies of Ceylon, they are the cornerstone of royal diplomacy and finance:

> the king sends them via his men to other kings, princes, and great lords – sometimes for tribute, sometimes for love – and also sells some in exchange for gold and silver. The king does this in order that his rubies be expensive and of great worth; for if he let other men mine it and take it throughout the world, they would extract them until they would be less expensive and of lesser worth. That is why the king has set such a high punishment – so no one extract any without his permission. (§47, p. 38)

To this account of balas rubies, Marco Polo adds: 'Know also, in truth . . . in this same country, in another mountain, are found the stones from which azure is made: this is the finest and best azure in the world' (§47, p. 38). This is lapis lazuli, absent from al-Nuwayrī's list but highly prized since antiquity. It has been unearthed in burial sites in northern Mesopotamia and in Upper Egypt from as early as the mid-fourth millennium BCE. In the medieval West, lapis lazuli was ground to a fine powder to produce the brilliant blue used in illuminated manuscripts; in the thirteenth century, technical innovations in the way the pigment was prepared allowed illuminators to produce a gradation of shades. In 2019 traces of lapis discovered in the dental calculus of a female monastic from eleventh- or twelfth-century northern Germany led researchers to reconsider women's roles in manuscript production.

Finally, jade, so central to Chinese artistic traditions, is never mentioned in the *Description* – striking confirmation that the

world Marco Polo seeks to describe to his audience is not China
but that of the Mongols.

Ceramics

> I tell you that in this province . . . are made porcelain
> bowls – large and small, the most beautiful you can
> imagine, made nowhere other than in this city; from
> there they are carried throughout the world. There
> are many great markets, so big that for a Venetian
> groat you could get 3 bowls so beautiful that no one
> could imagine better ones. (§157, p. 142)

This is the lone mention that Marco Polo makes of porcelain,
in connection with a city in the vicinity of the great southern
Chinese port of Zaytun (modern Quanzhou). The Old French
word he uses is *porcellaine*, otherwise found in the *Description* to
refer to the cowrie shells that circulated widely as currency across
the premodern world. For all his appreciation for their beauty,
he does not specify colours and, curiously, mentions only bowls
– not the jars, boxes, pillows or figures (human and animal)
characteristic of Chinese ceramics, nor the shapes typical of the
goods exported to the Islamic world.

Prized for its translucence, produced by a technique unknown
in the West until the eighteenth century, Chinese porcelain had
long been a luxury export to the Islamic world. In the anonymous
first part of *Accounts of China and India*, the Chinese are said to
have 'a fine type of clay that is made into cups as delicate as glass:
when held up to the light, any liquid in them can be seen through
the body of the cup, even though it is of clay.'[17] Archaeological
digs in Fustat (Old Cairo) have unearthed Chinese ceramics in
a variety of shapes, glazes, colours and quality. Such porcelains
were so popular in Persia that its artisans developed a type of
pottery called fritware in an attempt to imitate Chinese celadons

(illus. 41). Pieces found in Egypt and Iran differ in both form and function from wares made for domestic consumption, revealing the scale of a ceramics industry geared expressly for foreign markets. Indeed, porcelain (along with silk) was the main Chinese export to Southeast Asia (both mainland and insular) as well, where it was traded in exchange for spices, aromatics and exotic commodities like rhinoceros horn or elephant tusks from Khmer, Java (a transhipment point for the eastern Indonesian archipelago) and Champa (the coastal lowlands of central Vietnam).

Before the Mongol conquest, celadon ware from Longquan (southwest Zhejiang province) had reached a new height of

41 Glazed fritware bowl with three fishes, in imitation of Chinese celadon, Iran, c. 1300–1350.

refinement under the Southern Song: 'elegant, simple and well-proportioned forms sheathed in a wide range of thick, smooth, lustrous green glazes that look and feel like polished jade' (illus. 42).[18] In 1278, even before their conquest of the South was complete, the Mongols established a 'Porcelain Bureau' over the region. Muslim merchants in the port of Zaytun oversaw the export of wares from Jingdezhen, in the hills of the inland province of Jianxi; propitiously located near sources of raw materials and transport routes, it had long been a major production site and would reach its peak between 1295 and 1324 – precisely the period between Marco Polo's return to Venice and his death (illus. 43).

42 Stoneware dish with celadon glaze (Longquan ware) and relief decoration of fish, Yuan China, 13th century.

43 Foliated porcelain plate (Jingdezhen ware) with rocks, plants and melons, Yuan China, 14th century.

To understand the effusiveness of Marco Polo's brief appreciation of southern Chinese porcelain we have only to remember the *bacini* (plates and bowls) embedded in the facades of numerous churches in Rustichello's native Pisa (illus. 17). These ceramics came from the city's trading partners across the Islamic Mediterranean: green-and-brown ware from North Africa and al-Andalus (Muslim Iberia) (illus. 44), lustreware from Egypt (illus. 45) and stamped ware, also from al-Andalus. By and large these *bacini* dated from the eleventh century, when ceramics from the Muslim world were considerably more refined than their Latin European counterparts. By Marco's day, their quality had improved, in part

44 Tin-glaze green-and-brown Málaga ware, Basilica of San Piero
a Grado, Pisa.

through imitation of those imported models; nevertheless, it
would be several centuries before they could rival even pedestrian
examples of Chinese porcelain, 'so beautiful that no one could
imagine better ones' (§157, p. 142).

Conclusion

Around the same time that crusade apologist William of Adam
was condemning Italian merchants for seeking Indian luxuries
in the port of Alexandria, the encyclopaedist al-Nuwayrī wrote
of the same trade:

45 Egyptian lustreware basin, Church of San Sisto, Pisa.

It is said that India's sea is full of pearls, its mountains full
of rubies, its trees are all fragrant wood, its blossoms full
of perfume. The aromatic wood of India (aloewood) is
reckoned among the finest fragrances. Elephants are found
in India, along with rhinoceroses, tigers, peacocks, and
parrots. It possesses red rubies, white sandalwood, ivory,
different types of aromatic essences, clothing made of
velvet and other things, caps, and fabrics.[19]

Coming, like William of Adam, from the northern shores
of the Mediterranean, Marco Polo nevertheless inhabits a world

much closer to al-Nuwayrī's, reflecting the merchant's appreciation for the animal, vegetable and mineral luxuries of the Indies combined with the cosmopolitan experience of a servant of the Great Khan.

FIVE

Portrait Gallery:
Marco Polo's Contemporaries

In Chapter One, we began our exploration of the inter-
connectedness of late thirteenth-century Eurasia with the
observation that when St Francis of Assisi and Chinggis
Khan died in 1226 and 1227, respectively, the two inhabited
separate worlds. In the intervening chapters, we have explored
the complexity of Marco Polo's world through rubrics suggested
by *The Description of the World* itself: its two alternate titles, *The
Book of the Great Khan* and *The Book of Marvels*; and the commodities so systematically catalogued throughout Marco Polo's
chapters on Asia and the Indian Ocean system. In this final chapter, we return to the inspiration behind the pairing of St Francis
of Assisi and Chinggis Khan. Moving outside the bounds of
Marco Polo's book, we instead take the coincidence between
his lifespan (1254–1324) and that of three remarkable figures
– one from China, one from India and one from the Byzantine
Empire and Ilkhanate Persia – to add colour and depth to the
rich interconnected world of the second half of the thirteenth
century through the first quarter of the fourteenth century. Each
extraordinary in their own way, these individuals – a painter, a
poet and a patron of religious foundations – illuminate the cultural aspects of their world, too often absent from the political,
military and economic histories typical of studies on the Mongols,
their empire and the global Middle Ages.

Zhao Mengfu (1254–1322)

In 1287 a very handsome man of aristocratic bearing recently arrived at Qubilai's court caught the attention of the Great Khan:

> Emperor Shizu [Qubilai Khan] was pleased as soon as he saw him and commanded him to sit in a position superior to that of the minister of the left, Ye Li. Some said that it was inappropriate for Mengfu, a son of the Song imperial family, to be in such close proximity to the emperor, but the emperor would not hear their complaint. Indeed, the emperor immediately sent him to the Chancellery, commanding Mengfu to draft an edict to be promulgated to the nation. When the emperor read it, he was delighted and said: 'You have grasped what I had in mind to say.'[1]

This scene of the Great Khan taking special interest in a newcomer, an 'outstanding talent and a luminary character, a man who would not have been out of place among immortals', comes from the *Yuan Shi*. It bears a striking resemblance to Rustichello's account of Marco Polo's own arrival at Qubilai's court a dozen or so years before. But besides the difference in their ages on entering Mongol service, the distance between the two could hardly have been greater.

Zhau Mengfu, born into a family of scholar-officials in 1254, was a direct descendant of Taizu (d. 976), the founding emperor of the Song dynasty. His father Zhao Yuyin (1213–1265) had held important posts under the Southern Song, and young Mengfu had received the kind of traditional education that would have prepared him for a position in the imperial bureaucracy. Qubilai's conquest of the Southern Song Empire, however, turned this entire class of scholar-officials into 'leftover subjects' (*yimin*) occupying the bottom tier of the Mongols' four-part hierarchy.

Like other Southern Song loyalists who wanted nothing to do with the new regime centred in Dadu/Khanbaliq, Mengfu withdrew in a kind of self-imposed exile to his birthplace, Wuxing (present-day Huzhou), to the north of the former Southern Song capital of Hangzhou (Marco Polo's Quinsai). In this picturesque landscape on the southern shore of Lake Tai, a region known for its cultivation of arts and letters, he devoted himself to the traditional literati pastimes of study, painting and calligraphy.

Though Qubilai adopted a Chinese dynastic name, Yuan, in 1271, traditional historiography has typically emphasized the division between the Mongol conquerors and their erstwhile Southern Song 'leftover' subjects. But the lived reality of this transitional period was much more complex. With the Mongol conquest came an influx of administrators from the new regime, including northern Chinese and Central Asians who began mixing with members of the southern elite around typical literati activities like art collecting and connoisseurship, as we see attested in some of Zhao Mengfu's poems and colophons. Then in 1286 he was one of twenty southerners expressly recruited for imperial service. He relocated to Dadu/Khanbaliq the following year, a move that occasioned the interview recorded at the beginning of this section.

Given Mengfu's status as *wangsun* – a 'prince descendant' of the Sung imperial house – his arrival in Dadu would have contributed to the prestige and credibility of Mongol rule. But equally valuable to the Yuan regime were his talents as a scholar-official. Initially he was invited to serve in the Hanlin Academy – the imperial secretariat (dating back to the Tang dynasty) responsible for transcribing old texts (including Buddhist and Daoist sutras) and composing new ones, such as inscriptions on commemorative stelae or official pronouncements (like the edict whose wording gained him Qubilai's favour). He was also appointed to the Ministry of War, the department overseeing the famed postal service, the *yam*. Over the next few years, Zhao Mengfu shuttled frequently between Dadu and the south on government business. Such trips afforded him ample opportunities to cultivate an expanding network of like-minded artists and scholars for whom poetry, painting and other cultural artefacts were the privileged objects of conversation and exchange. In one sense, Mengfu enjoyed a meteoric rise, consulting on major policy issues and eventually earning the confidence of one of the Great Khan's senior advisors, Arghun Sali. At the same time, his term in imperial service was turbulent. He repeatedly clashed with Qubilai's chief minister, Sangha (who fell from favour and was executed in 1291). A poem entitled 'My Crime in Leaving' expresses the tension between the 'far-reaching ambition' that seduced him into the 'dusty net' of imperial service and the attractions of the 'mountains', 'hills and valleys' and 'southern clouds' of home: 'Once I was a gull on the water; now I am a bird in a cage.'[2]

In the 1290s, the decade bracketed by the Polos' departure from China and Marco's composition of the *Description*, Zhao Mengfu bounced between different postings and shuttled in and out of imperial service, reflecting his discomfiture at serving the Mongols as well as the political instability of the times. In 1292, wanting to leave the capital, Zhao secured an appointment in Jinan (in modern Shandong province); in 1295, the year after Qubilai's death, he was summoned back to the capital to help compile the *Veritable Records* of his reign. That task complete, he withdrew to Wuxing on the grounds of ill-health. A poem penned that same year suggests, however, that health was not the only reason for his retirement:

> The lake fish longs for its home spring,
> The caged beast longs for its old wilds.
> So, the official in government is bound by ties:
> He goes to work early, always finishes late.

Paperwork to handle, managing schedules and meetings;
What's the use in handing on the imperishable?
A decade I have served this social end,
Dust and dirt now fill my clothes.[3]

Indeed, he was a reluctant bureaucrat; as his official biography in the *Yuan Shi* put it, 'Mengfu delayed his return to office for a long time.' In 1297 he was appointed to a provincial governorship that he did not take up. In 1298 he, along with other prominent calligraphers, 'received an imperial command to transcribe the Buddhist Tripitaka [ancient scriptures] in gold ink'. He then declined an appointment to the Hanlin Academy that he had been offered as a reward, preferring to return to the south.

In his retirement, Zhao Mengfu devoted himself to the life of a *literatus*, maintaining a lively interchange with fellow painters and poets. A diary kept by his younger contemporary, the painter, collector and art connoisseur Guo Bi (1280–c. 1335), gives a flavour of the social life shared among such scholar-officials in their rural retreats. Visiting each other's homes, taking excursions to local monasteries (both Taoist and Buddhist), sailing on nearby waterways, indulging in food liberally accompanied by drink, he and his friends shared drawings and poems. (Guo's own surviving corpus consists of eleven ink-on-paper handscrolls featuring misty mountain landscapes and bamboo – favourite topics, as we will see, of Zhao Mengfu's wife, Guan Daosheng.) Such works were often spontaneously composed for the occasion, as reflected in this entry from the sixth month, twelfth day: 'After dinner, I accompanied the others to Perfect Truth Daoist Monastery, where we sat under four catalpa trees to catch some breeze. I wrote twenty wine poems for Zhao Boqian.' On the following day, Guo 'painted a picture of an impressive stone for Mr. Zhao . . . Its shape was very unusual and yet no trace of a chisel could be detected. It was as though it had been carved by fairies.'

On hot, mosquito-plagued days that give way to evenings made pleasant by cool breezes and silvery moonlight, diary entries – punctuated with mentions of getting drunk on wine – record Guo making numerous scrolls of calligraphy along with paintings or drawings of orchids, bamboo and 'two old trees', all at the behest of friends, whose requests are often accompanied by gifts of paper suited to the purpose. Guo's throwaway comment on his rain-soaked boat ride home – 'All the riders were common people, so there was no one to talk to' – reveals the rarefied air of privilege that he and his companions inhabited.[4]

For Zhao Mengfu, the second half of the 1290s was an intense period of artistic production. Two of his best-known works date from the year 1296, both ink-and-colour on paper handscrolls roughly 30 centimetres (12 in.) high: *Horse and Groom* (illus. 46), today in the Metropolitan Museum of Art in New York, and *Man Riding* (illus. 47), in the Palace Museum in Beijing. These are

46 Zhao Mengfu, *Horse and Groom*, 1296, handscroll (detail), ink and colours on paper.

47 Zhao Mengfu, *Man Riding*, 1296, handscroll (detail), ink and colours on paper.

appealing and apparently simple images whose main figure is sometimes taken as a self-portrait of the artist, or, in the latter example, as a portrait of his younger brother Zhao Mengyu. In fact, they exemplify the dense nexus of social, cultural and personal associations characterizing much of Mengfu's work. Depictions of horses had a long history in Chinese culture. Especially resonant was the legend of Bole and Jiufang Gao, two ancient sages celebrated as excellent judges of horses, often used as an allegory for the ability to identify talented officials. On the one hand, *Horse and Groom* places the viewer in the position of judge, asking us to recognize Mengfu's talent in discharging his official duties. At the same time, the plump horse and poised and confident groom implicitly set this picture in conversation with works by two of Zhao Mengfu's contemporaries: Gong Kai (1222–1307), whose *Emaciated Horse* (illus. 48) allegorizes the degraded state of the country under Mongol rule; and Ren Renfa (1254–1327), whose handscroll *Two Horses* (illus. 49) – one fat and one thin – represents (according to his colophon) the contrast between 'chaste' and 'profligate' officials. *Man Riding*, from the same year,

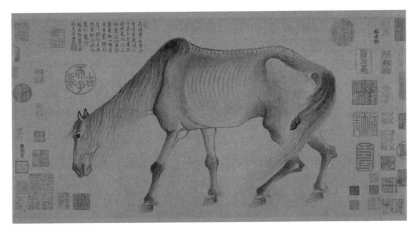

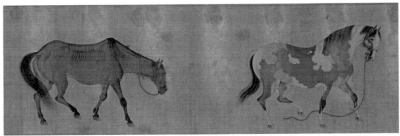

48 Gong Kai, *Emaciated Horse*, Yuan dynasty, handscroll (detail),
ink on paper.
49 Ren Renfa, *Two Horses*, Yuan dynasty, handscroll (detail),
ink and colours on silk.

depicts a scholar-official on his way to taking up his post. A back-
and-forth exchange between Zhao and his younger brother
preserved in a series of colophons on the scroll's mounting and
backing bring to light the artist's conception of his own talent
and his self-conscious relationship with earlier masters. As Mengfu
recounts: 'Since I was young I have loved painting horses, but it
was not until I actually got to see three genuine handscroll paintings of horses by Han Gan that I first grasped its [higher] purpose'
(illus. 50). As these were Tang-era works that Mengfu likely first
saw in Dadu, *Man Riding* reveals the way his decision to enter

Mongol service not only suggested new themes for his painting
but provided new stylistic models that spurred transformations
in his own art. His return to Wuxing in 1295 probably also led
Mengfu to reintroduce these earlier artists and styles to his network of southern colleagues, previously cut off from such parts
of their cultural heritage by the political divisions between
Cathay in the north (under the rule not only of the Mongols but
of their Jin-Jurchen predecessors) and the empire of the Southern
Song.

Among the literati that Zhao Mengfu would have frequented
during his time in the south was his father's friend Zhou Mi,
author of the vivid account of the social life of Quinsai quoted
in Chapter Two. In his *Record of Clouds and Mists Passing Before
One's Eyes*, Zhou Mi catalogued 43 items in Zhao Mengfu's

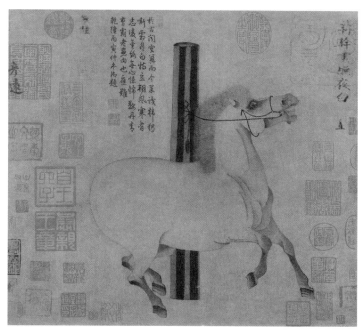

50 Han Gan, *Night-Shining White*, c. 750, handscroll (detail),
ink on paper.

personal art collection. These included works by old masters from the turbulent tenth-century Five Dynasties and Ten Kingdoms period, known for their depiction of birds and flowers, like Huang Quan (later Shu), and landscapes of southern China, like Dong Yuan (southern Tang); the late eleventh-century Northern Song master Li Gonglin, whose paintings of horses strongly influenced Mengfu and his contemporaries; and Zhao Mengjian (d. *c.* 1267), another descendant of the first Song emperor, who was known for his depiction of bamboo, old trees and flowers. Mengfu must have especially prized those parts of his collection associated with the Northern Song emperor Huizong, a talented artist and enthusiastic collector, albeit a weak emperor who had abdicated in the face of the Jin conquest of 1126 and died in captivity. Mengfu owned one painting, *Crows in an Old Tree with Young Bamboo*, by the emperor himself and two pieces (one calligraphic scroll and one painting) that he had inscribed. Another painting, *The Knight Errant of Wuling* by the eighth-century Tang dynasty artist Han Gan, was inscribed by the twelfth-century Song emperor Gaozong. Two handscrolls in Zhao Mengfu's collection are of particular interest since they survive today: *Five Oxen*, attributed to the eighth-century Tang dynasty artist Han Huang (though possibly a thirteenth-century copy) (illus. 51); and *Mist Descending on the Dense Forest* by the aforementioned Zhao Mengjian, now in the Metropolitan Museum of Art under the title *Narcissus* (illus. 52). Rounding out Zhao's collection

were several decorative objects: a hairpin and bracelets of white jade, bronze vessels, and an incense burner and various carved stone inkstones.[5]

Thanks to Zhou Mi's catalogue annotations and to the colophons inscribed on various handscrolls, we are able to reconstruct the 'biographies' of certain objects in Zhao Mengfu's collection in astonishing detail, matched by few objects produced in thirteenth-century Europe. Zhou Mi records that a small ceremonial brazier (*ding*) with gold filigree inlay in Mengfu's possession had originally belonged to Jia Sidao (the Southern Song chancellor assassinated in 1275, just ahead of the Mongol conquest); he had given it to Empress Dowager Xie, the regent who eventually surrendered the capital to the Mongols in 1276 and lived out the remainder of her life in exile in Dadu under the protection of Qubilai's chief wife Chabi. After that, the *ding* 'fell into the hands of a Korean merchant who sold it to Hu Yong', a Southern Song official who rose to high rank under the Yuan; known for his generosity and hospitality (including towards commoners), Hu was a connoisseur especially attracted (to judge by Zhou Mi's account of his collection) by fine jade objects.

Han Huang's *Five Oxen* bears three colophons by Zhao Mengfu. The first lists the five paintings by Han that he has seen; it names two of the handscroll's previous owners, the second of whom had

51 Han Huang, *Five Oxen*, Tang dynasty, handscroll (detail), ink and colours on paper.

52 Zhao Mengjian, *Narcissus*, mid-13th century, handscroll (detail), ink on paper.

given it to him as a gift after he had enquired about buying it. The second colophon reads the work as an allusion to an earlier sixth-century painting of two oxen, one wearing a golden halter and one grazing freely – an allegory of the dilemma of whether or not to enter imperial service (akin to the Aesopian fable of the conversation between the well-fed but shackled dog and the starving but free-ranging wolf). Mengfu's engagement with *Five Oxen* was thus particularly complex: his antiquarian interest in Han mirrors Han's own antiquarian interest in the older work; Mengfu later took one of Han's oxen as a model for one of the figures in his own 1301 painting *Old Trees, Grazing Horses* (illus. 54); and the allusion, once removed, to the earlier 'two oxen' portrait anticipates Mengfu's frequent use of animals to express the ethical dilemmas faced by Song literati under Mongol rule, as in his famous handscroll *Sheep and Goat* (c. 1300–1305), today in the National Museum of Asian Art in Washington, DC (illus. 53). By 1314 *Five Oxen* was in the collection of the Crown Prince – presumably a gift from Mengfu after he returned to imperial service under Emperor Ayurbarwada in 1311. The biographies of these two objects thus exemplify Mengfu's close ties to both the Southern Song and Yuan imperial families.

Zhao Mengfu's relationship with Zhou Mi went beyond their shared interest in art and art collecting. In 1295 after leaving Mongol service, he painted a handscroll entitled *Autumn Colours on the Qiao and Hua Mountains* (illus. 55), today in the National Palace Museum in Taipei. The mountains in question were located north of Jinan, the provincial capital where Zhao had spent the previous three years; this area was the ancestral home of Zhou Mi, who had never seen it in person. As Zhao wrote on the handscroll: 'After I left office and returned home, I made [Zhou Mi] discuss the mountains and rivers of [Shangdong] with me.' Mount Hua, he notes, is well known through an ancient text called the *Zuozhuan*; 'In shape it has a high peak and distinctive posture and is unusual enough that I made this picture to show it to him.'[6] Mengfu's experiences in the government of the Yuan conquerors allow him literally to paint a picture for Zhou Mi of the ancestral homeland he has never seen.

Beyond these glimpses of literati culture, our spotlight on Zhao Mengfu illuminates the life and work of his wife, Guan Daosheng (1262–1319), an important poet and painter in her

53 Zhao Mengfu, *Sheep and Goat*, *c.* 1300–1305, handscroll (detail), ink on paper.

54 Zhao Mengfu, *Old Trees, Grazing Horses*, 1301, handscroll, ink on paper.

own right. The pair married in 1286, just before Mengfu's initial departure for Dadu. She came from a distinguished family, and the two had long seemed destined for each other, as Zhao later wrote in her epitaph:

> Her father was Guan Shen, . . . known for his exceptional talent and unconventionality, and his chivalrous conduct

was the talk of the neighborhood. My wife since birth had
intelligence that surpassed others. Her father cherished
her, definitely wanting to get a fine son-in-law. Her father
and I were from the same district, and because he also
had a high regard for me, I knew that someday she would
become my wife.[7]

Guan came into her own as an artist during the period of the
couple's retreat to Wuxing: of the 33 works, extant or copied,
attributed to her in the catalogue of a 1988 exhibition of female
Chinese artists, the earliest dates from 1296 – the same year as
Zhao's *Horse and Groom* and *Man Riding*.

The only extant painting securely attributed to Guan
Daosheng is *Bamboo Groves in Mist and Rain* (illus. 56), dated
to 1308 and bearing an inscription dedicating it to a 'Lady of the
Qu Kingdom'. Guan would become known as one of the four

55 Zhao Mengfu, *Autumn Colours on the Qiao and Hua Mountains*,
1295, handscroll (detail), ink and colours on paper.

greatest bamboo artists of the early Yuan. Bamboo – often referred
to as 'this gentleman' from an anecdote about a fourth-century
calligrapher who planted bamboo in his garden in order to
have 'this gentleman' for company – was hugely resonant in the
Chinese tradition. As the eleventh-century late Northern Song
poet and calligrapher Su Shi had quipped, 'want of meat makes
one skinny, but want of bamboo makes one vulgar; a person who
is skinny may yet fill out, but a vulgar scholar cannot be rem-
edied!'[8] Interest in bamboo intensified in the early fourteenth
century: in 1307, the year preceding Guan's *Bamboo Groves*, the
painter Li Kan published a *Treatise on Bamboo*, a study of different species of bamboo from all around China, illustrated with
woodblock prints. These associations gave bamboo a distinctly
masculine cast. A colophon written by Guan's elder sister on an
ink-on-silk handscroll dated to 1309 (today in the Boston Museum
of Fine Arts) recounts:

> While peacefully sitting in the Gentleman's
> Studio, Madam said, 'Since "Gentleman" is the
> name of the studio, why is there no bamboo?'
> Thereupon, an attendant was asked to grind
> ink, and she sketched this branch in the middle
> of the studio . . . On another day, when my

56 Guan Daosheng, *Bamboo Groves in Mist and Rain*, 1308, handscroll (detail), ink on paper.

brother-in-law [Zhao Mengfu] will come to look [at this painting], I will ask him to write his inscription.'[9]

The following year, Guan herself wrote on a handscroll of bamboo: 'To play with brush and ink is a masculine sort of thing to do, yet I made this painting. Wouldn't someone say that I have transgressed [propriety]? How despicable; how despicable.'[10]

Where Marco Polo largely disappears from view after 1298, when he and Rustichello of Pisa composed the *Description*, Zhao Mengfu remained active through the first two decades of the fourteenth century. He spent the years between 1300 and 1309 in Hangzhou as the superintendent of Confucian education for Jiangzhe, the province south of the Yangtze River; there he continued to paint, compose poetry and tomb inscriptions, write colophons on others' work and collect theirs on his. Then in 1310 Qubilai's great-grandson, the Confucian-educated crown prince Ayurbarwada, summoned Mengfu back to the capital. After succeeding his brother as emperor the following year, he devoted his reign (1311–20) to promoting traditional Chinese culture, sponsoring the circulation of Chinese books and, most importantly, reinstituting the Confucian-based civil service exam system that had been abolished by his predecessors. He awarded prestigious positions and commissions to scholars and painters, culminating in 1316 when Zhao Mengfu was named director of the Hanlin Academy. As his *Yuan Shi* official biography records, 'the emperor regarded him with deep affection' and when 'discussing scholars of great literary talent with his attendant ministers', compared him to noted Tang and Song dynasty figures. 'On another occasion, the emperor called him a model of constancy and probity, a scholar of broad learning, an incomparable artist and [an adept] who had fathomed the precepts of Buddhism and Daoism – surpassing others in every case.'[11] Guan Daosheng also received recognition: Ayurbarwada awarded her the title 'lady of Wuxing' and commissioned a scroll 'to make posterity aware that in our court there was a Lady that excelled in calligraphy'; subsequently he ordered Mengfu and their son Zhao Yong to join examples of their work to hers so that later generations would know of this 'one family, all strong [in] calligraphy . . . an extraordinary thing'.[12]

Remembered today for his paintings, Zhao Mengfu was also a poet and an accomplished musician who collected antique instruments. But calligraphy was central to his world. Both in his career as an administrator and in his private life as a scholar and connoisseur, experimentation with different calligraphic styles became a vehicle for adapting to changing historical conditions. Coming of age as an imperial scion in the waning years of the Southern Song, Zhao's earliest brushwork reflected the influence of his imperial forebears. However, after the Mongol conquest and his move, in the 1290s, into the Yuan bureaucracy, he adopted stylistic features from the Tang, the powerful early seventh- through early tenth-century dynasty whose Central Asian antecedents made them, like the Yuan, open to foreign exchange and influence; then, from the early 1300s, he turned to Northern Song styles, culminating a lifetime of negotiating the vicissitudes of the reigns of Qubilai and his three successors over an eventful and productive career.

But the favour shown to Zhao Mengfu by the emperor attracted the jealousy and resentment of some of his colleagues, and when his wife fell ill, Mengfu secured permission for them to return home. Guan Daosheng, however, died en route (in 1319); Mengfu, now in his late sixties, heavily mourned her loss. Penning a note of thanks to a venerable Buddhist monk who had sent disciples to preside over rituals marking the second anniversary of her death, he wrote: 'My late wife definitely has a hope of being reborn in Heaven, and this would not have been possible if not for the kindness of you, our teacher. As I humbly write this letter to you, I am overcome by the extent of my grief.' For the remaining three years of his own life, Zhao, who before this had painted bamboo only sporadically (including on a hand-scroll done in collaboration with Guan in 1299), now devoted most of his paintings to his wife's favourite topic. Examples include a hanging scroll entitled *Old Tree, Bamboo and Rock* and his last known work, *Elegance Emerging from a Bamboo Thicket*.[13] Zhao Mengfu died at home in Wuxing in 1322.

Amīr Khusrau (1253–1325)

Like Zhao Mengfu, Amīr Khusrau (or Khusraw) was an exact contemporary of Marco Polo. He spent his life in the Delhi sultanate, a Muslim empire founded in the late twelfth century by Turkic conquerors linked to the Ghurid sultanate (in today's eastern Persia and Afghanistan). Khusrau's father came from near Balkh, the great Silk Road city in present-day Afghanistan; fleeing south ahead of Chinggis Khan's campaigns of conquest in the early 1220s, he entered the service of Iltutmish (d. 1236), founder of the Delhi sultanate. His mother came from an

important Delhi family, also in Iltutmish's service. By the time
Khusrau was born, Delhi was a cosmopolitan place,

> renowned throughout the Islamic world for its institutions
> of learning and as a haven for wandering scholars and
> poets . . . The indigenous population consisted chiefly
> of Hindus, Jains, and two broad categories of Muslims:
> Indian converts and immigrants from Central Asia who
> had settled there as refugees or were attracted by the
> centres of learning . . . Such institutions also attracted
> Sufis, and Delhi's thriving markets also brought in
> merchants and traders.[14]

Like many medieval figures, Amīr Khusrau was a polymath
who wrote in both Persian (the court language not only of the
sultanate but across a wide swathe of Central and West Asia)
and Hindavi (the vernacular language of Delhi). A fourteenth-
century biographical sketch recounts that on the day of his birth,
a madman predicted that he would become the most eminent
of poets. Both his father (who died young) and his maternal
grandfather, himself a patron of letters, provided Khusrau with
an excellent education; however, his fascination for poetry often
distracted him from more formal instruction. As he later recalled,
'I began to compose verses and *ghazals* that roused the admiration
and wonder of my elders.'[15] With Delhi's other most prominent
poet, Amīr Hasan, Khusrau became a follower of the charismatic
Sufi shaikh Nizam al-Din Auliya. His verses were known and admired across the Persianate world, even earning praise from the
era's towering poet, Sa'di of Shiraz, from the province of Fars in
southwestern Persia.

Khusrau lived in an age of political turmoil that saw rule of
the Delhi sultanate pass from one dynasty to another. He came
of age during the reign of Sultan Ghiyath al-Din Balban, a former

slave who had seized power at the death of Iltutmish's son Nasir al-Din. His twenty-year rule (1266–87) provided some measure of stability at the outset of Khusrau's literary career, in an era punctuated by succession crises at the end of nearly every reign. A Sanskrit inscription carved on a well outside Delhi in 1276 praised Balban (in a list integrating the Delhi sultans into a roster of local rulers, both native and foreign) as 'the central gem in the pearl necklace of the seven sea-girt earth'. The inscription, which had opened with salutations to the Hindu gods Ganapati (Ganesha) and Śiva, went on to catalogue Balban's military victories before concluding that 'Vishnu himself . . . taking Lakshmi on his breast, and relinquishing all worries, sleeps in peace on the ocean of milk' – high praise since Vishnu is the god whose incarnations appear in times of crisis.[16] Balban's dynasty, however, did not long survive his death. His grandson and successor Qaiqabad reigned for only three years before being overthrown in 1290. The new ruler, the septuagenarian Jalal al-Din Khalaji (r. 1290–96), was overthrown in turn by his nephew, 'Ala al-Din. Though ruthless, his twenty-year reign (1296–1316) provided another stretch of stability, but when he died, the previous pattern repeated itself. His son and successor Qutb al-Din ruled only briefly (1316–20); and at his death, Ghiyath al-Din Tughluq (r. 1320–25) seized power, inaugurating yet another new dynasty that lasted until 1413.

Where Marco Polo spent all his time in Asia under the regime of Qubilai Khan (r. 1260–94), Amīr Khusrau weathered all of the Delhi sultanate's political upheavals and regime changes by transferring his poetic services from one prince to another, attaching himself to the courts and travelling retinues of successive royal patrons. Beginning in 1272, not yet twenty years old, Khusrau had attracted the patronage of Balban's nephew, spending two years as a favoured court poet, then of Balban's sons Bughra Khan, the governor of Bengal, and Muhammad, the heir apparent and governor of Multan. Muhammad died fighting the Mongols in a battle in which Khusrau himself was briefly taken captive.

Khusrau's literary output was prodigious; as his fourteenth-century biographer put it, 'Libraries became filled with books written by him' in Persian, and in multiple genres.[17] Best remembered today are his *ghazals* (lyric love poems or songs in the Sufi tradition) and his *Quintet* (*Khamsa*), adaptations of five celebrated verse romances by the twelfth-century Persian master Nizami Ganjavi (d. 1209). Many of his works, however, were occasional pieces written for or in praise of his various patrons: panegyric odes (*qasīdas*), which include a long poem composed in 1289 commemorating Sultan Qaiqabad's reconciliation with his father (Khusrau's former patron) Bughra Khan; an account of 1291 of the victories of Jalal al-Din Khalaji; and an elegy on the death of 'Ala al-Din, written in 1316.

At about the same time that Zhao Mengfu was preparing his final retreat from Mongol imperial service, Amīr Khusrau completed *The Nine Skies* (*Nuh-Sipihr*), a work in nine chapters, each in a different metre, celebrating the reign of the Khalaji sultan Qutb al-Din Malik Shah. Opening with a panegyric of the sultan, it recounts his accession to the throne and praises the glories of Delhi, especially the palace and congregational mosque constructed by Qutb al-Din. Later chapters include wisdom on statecraft and morality directed at the sultan (widely known for his dissolute behaviour) and members of different strata of society; accounts of one of the sultan's hunting expeditions and the birth of his son and descriptions of different seasonal festivals. It concludes with the author's celebration of his own poetic skills.

Of most interest to us is the third of Amīr Khusrau's nine chapters: an extended description of India in a new verse form of the author's own invention, designed to vaunt its superiority over such places as 'Rum' or Rome (as Byzantine and then Seljuq

Anatolia was called in both Persian and Arabic), Khurasan and Khotan (an ancient Buddhist kingdom in the present-day Chinese autonomous region of Xinjiang). Why does he prefer India over all other countries? Because it is his homeland, and because his spiritual master, the Sufi shaikh Nizam al-Din Auliya, has made it 'the centre of the world's attraction'.[18] India is 'Paradise on Earth', Khusrau opines, first of all for its climate. He contrasts its warmth with the 'singularly tortuous' summer heat of Arabia and especially the 'bitter cold' of winters in Khurasan, setting it apart both from the birthplace of Islam and from the seat of the Ghurid dynasty, former masters of the Delhi sultanate's founders. In contrast to places like Ray (ancient capital of the pre-Islamic Parthian Empire, near present-day Tehran) or Rum, where fragrant flowers do not grow except for two or three months, 'flowers here blossom the year round and they are all fragrant.' Fruits like mangoes, guavas and grapes; spices like cardamom, camphor and cloves; and the two 'rare delicacies' of bananas and betel leaves also flourish in India's climate. Its distinctive fauna includes birds, like the parrots that 'speak like human beings', repeating whatever they hear, from verses of the Qur'an to prayers to God, and the 'rare and beautiful' peacock – reminding us of Marco Polo's version of the death of St Thomas the Apostle, accidentally shot by an idolator hunting peacocks![19]

Though a devout Muslim, Amīr Khusrau's love for his homeland inspires an openness towards and admiration of India's non-Muslim peoples and culture. Notably, he praises the intellectual learning of the Brahmans: 'Though there are men of letters in other countries, nowhere is Wisdom or Philosophy better written than India.' Excepting only Islamic law (*fiqh*), all branches of learning, including logic, astrology and poetry, are found there, and it was the birthplace of natural sciences, mathematics and geography. Amīr Khusrau calls special attention to a curious trio of 'three arts' that have spread far beyond India, becoming, he says, 'popular adornments in every respectable household in the world': mathematics (including the concept of zero, an Indian innovation); *Kalīla and Dimnā*, derived from the Sanskrit tale collection, the *Panchatantra* – 'such a marvellous and meaningful work [that] it has been translated into Persian, Turkish, Arabic and Darī'; and the game of chess, 'a unique contribution of India to the world . . . Foreigners have tried to outdo India in this game but they could not compete and, humbly, they had to confess their inferiority.'[20]

Like Marco Polo, Amīr Khusrau marvels at the wonders and curiosities to be found among Hindus: magicians who can revive the dead, extend their lifespan by controlling their breathing ('because everybody has his fixed quota of breaths'), assume animal form, exert mind control on others, fly like birds, remain underwater at great length, control rainclouds and become invisible. 'Some of these are facts of magic,' he writes, 'and some are stories.' Like Marco Polo, he reports that a Hindu woman 'burns herself for her husband' and a Hindu man 'sacrifices his life for his deity or his chieftain'. Although such self-sacrifice 'is not allowed by the religion of Islam', Khusrau astonishingly calls it 'a great and noble deed', opining that if lawful for Muslims, 'good people would have sacrificed their life with pleasure'.[21]

Nothing better illustrates the richness and diversity of India than the plurality of languages found there. For Khusrau, this begins with the three languages of Islam: Arabic, Persian and Turkic, 'like pearls on the face of the earth', each having originated 'from a place of its own' before having 'spread all over the world'. Arabic, naturally enough, holds pride of place; 'the language of scholars' governed by 'fixed and set rules' of grammar and usage that must be 'regularly observed for reading religious books like the Qur'an and other books of sciences', it requires assiduous study to learn and maintain:

Unless one works hard for a lifetime to acquire proficiency in speech, he cannot ably and correctly read even a single leaf of the Arabic.

It is not because he is dull or [a] fool but because one should possess extraordinary enlightenment and stamina to learn the Arabic.[22]

Then there is Persian, 'a very sweet language with its centre around Shiraz' that had become the courtly lingua franca across the eastern Islamic world. Unlike Arabic, limited by its difficulty to the scholarly elite, Persian spread readily among commoners. Khusrau, who composed most of his works in that language, gives a strikingly pragmatic explanation of why – though it lacks 'a grammar of its own' – he has never attempted to compose one: 'The worth of a commodity depends upon its purchasers. If there is no demand, it is worthless.'[23] Third among the Islamic tongues is Turkic, which spread from its Central Asian homeland with Turkish rule. As it was the language of the ruling political and military elite, scholars compiled dictionaries and grammars for the nobles and army officers who were 'fascinated' by the language and used it 'for formal official business'.[24]

The glory of Arabic, Persian and Turkic, says Khusrau, comes from their vast geographical range. Although other languages may be 'also very beautiful', they 'are neither so sweet nor so enlightening' as these three linguistic 'pearls' since they are 'limited within the boundaries of their own land and . . . have not spread out' – a close parallel to the way Marco Polo and Rustichello of Pisa's contemporaries chose to write in French because 'the French language has spread all over the world, and is the most delightful to read and hear above any other.'[25] A contrary rationale takes over, however, as Khusrau pivots to a discussion of native Indian languages, noteworthy for their diversity: 'There is a different language in every corner of this land with its own system and technique,' corresponding to Marco Polo's enumeration of the many South Asian coastal cities and kingdoms that each have 'a language of their own'. Khusrau goes on to list a dozen regional vernaculars; all of these, he continues, 'are Hindawi languages since olden times . . . spoken by the people at large'. In addition, however, there is another language which is 'the best of all': Sanskrit, 'the language of the Brahmans'. Like Arabic, it has 'grammar, definitions, system, technique and rules, and literature', including 'four religious books' (the *Vedas*) containing 'all arts and sciences'. Sanskrit, Khusrau concludes, is 'a pearl among pearls. It may be inferior to Arabic but it is decidedly superior to the best of the Persian.' Finally, as he had previously pointed out, whereas 'the people of India speak different languages . . . people outside India – Chinese, Mongols, Turks and Arabs – 'cannot speak in Indian dialects'.[26]

In fact, alongside his prodigious corpus of Persian writings, Khusrau also composed in Hindavi – the vernacular precursor to modern Hindi. While never formally gathered together in his lifetime, verses attributed to him circulated orally and were collected in print in the eighteenth and nineteenth centuries. Some of these are devotional poems to his Sufi spiritual guide, Nizam al-Din Auliya; others are playful riddle poems, like the following:

> He visits my town once a year.
> He fills my mouth with kisses and nectar.
> I spend all my money on him.
> *Who, girl, your man?*
> No, a mango.[27]

He even mixes Persian and Hindavi in a bilingual, cross-register poem that provides a window onto the linguistic complexity of late thirteenth- and early fourteenth-century Delhi, typical of the dynamic linguistic and cultural interactions so widespread across Marco Polo's world.[28]

Amīr Khusrau's final years coincided with the short five-year reign of Ghiyath al-Din Tughluq, founder of the third ruling dynasty in the poet's lifetime. It was a turbulent time. The new sultan was a military commander over seventy years old. Together with his son, he undertook a series of campaigns to subdue break-away parts of the empire that had asserted their autonomy during the turmoil of the previous reign. The two waged successful campaigns in Bengal and against the Kakatiya kingdom (mentioned in the *Description* §175). But the sultan was killed in an apparently freak accident during their triumphal celebration in Delhi – a 'mishap' in which his son, Muhammad bin Tughluq, was suspected of complicity. During the latter's long reign (1325–51), the Delhi sultanate grew larger than any previous Indian state before contracting again by the time of his death.

Amīr Khusrau, however, did not live to see it. When Nizam al-Din Auliya, his spiritual guide, died, his biographer tells us, he 'blackened his face, tore his shirt, and rolling on the ground', predicted that he himself had not long to live. In fact, Khusrau died six months later; he was buried at the far end of his mentor's garden, having survived Marco Polo by a year – like our final subject, the Byzantine princess and Mongol khatun Maria Palaiologina.[29]

Maria Palaiologina (c. 1253–1325)

Our final contemporary, Maria Palaiologina, leaves much less trace in the historical record, yet what little we know of her is tantalizing. She was an illegitimate daughter of the Byzantine emperor Michael VIII Palaiologos of Nicaea, one of the rump states spawned in the aftermath of the Fourth Crusaders' conquest of Constantinople in 1204, who, in 1265, when she was about twelve, sent her as a bride to Hülegü (Qubilai's brother), conqueror of Baghdad and the Ilkhan of Persia. By the time she reached the Ilkhanate, however, Hülegü had died, so she was married instead to his son and successor Abaqa. When he died some seventeen years later, she returned to Constantinople, became a nun and founded a monastery informally dubbed 'Saint Mary of the Mongols' in her honour.

Maria's marriage was part of a series of political realignments that had played a large role in the Polos' own travels. In 1260, when Marco's father and uncle had set out from Constantinople on their first journey into Asia (*Description* §2), the Byzantine Empire had been ruled since 1204 by a line of 'Latin' (Western Christian) emperors descended from the counts of Flanders. The following year, however, Baldwin II was ousted by Michael VIII Palaiologos. His accession, as we have seen, spelled the downturn for the Venetians, close allies of the Latin emperors, in favour of his allies and their arch-rivals the Genoese. Thus it is no accident that when the elder Polos returned from their first journey to Qubilai's court in 1269, they travelled not through Constantinople, their original point of departure, but through the crusader outpost at Acre, where the Venetians still maintained a large colony. Restored to power but surrounded by a mosaic of competing, potentially hostile states, Michael VIII set to work on the diplomatic front, using his daughters to forge a spate of dynastic alliances.

His legitimate daughters were given in marriage to neighbouring Christian rulers: Eudokia to John II Grand Komnenos, the emperor of Trebizond (another rump Byzantine state); Eirene to Ivan III Asen, the tsar of Bulgaria; and Anna to Demetrios, son of the despot of Epiros. The two greatest regional powers, however, were Mongols: the khanate of the Golden Horde (Marco Polo's 'Tartars of the West'), ruled by descendants of Chinggis Khan's eldest son Jochi; and the Ilkhanate (Marco's 'Tartars of

57 Donor portrait of Maria Palaiologina, Kariye Mosque, Istanbul.

the East'), established by Hülegü following his conquest of
Baghdad (1258). To these non-Christian rulers, Michael gave
his illegitimate daughters: Euphrosyne to Nogay, khan of the
westernmost part of the Golden Horde, west of the Black Sea,
and Maria to Abaqa.

In the Ilkhanate, Maria entered a world in which royal women
famously exercised considerable influence. She became known
by the honorific 'Despina Khatun', which combined the Greek
word for 'lady' with the Mongol title for queen. Though the khans
were polygamous, each khatun had her own household; as Marco
Polo remarks of Qubilai's four wives, 'They are called empresses

and each is called by her name; each of these ladies has a court of her own' (§82, p. 72). Given the Mongols' tolerance for different religions, Maria kept her Orthodox faith, arriving in the Ilkhanid capital of Tabriz accompanied by a high-ranking abbot of the Pantokrator monastery in Constantinople and bringing a tent highly decorated with silken images, presumably to serve as a chapel. As khatun, she served as protector and sponsor of local Christians, who were principally 'Nestorians' (that is, adherents of the Church of the East), but also promoted Orthodox Christianity, commissioning a church in northern Iraq decorated by an artist imported from the Byzantine capital.

After Abaqa's death in 1282, Maria returned to Constantinople, now ruled by her half-brother, Andronikos II. Over the

58 Church of Saint Mary of the Mongols (*Kanlı Kilise* or Bloody Church), Istanbul.

next decade or so, even as the Ilkhanate was destabilized by a series of succession disputes (reported in §§202–16 of the *Description*), Maria remained in touch with her in-laws. She was able to obtain the cross of the great fourth-century saint Gregory the Illuminator from her late husband's nephew Baidu (r. 1295), and several years later served as intermediary in seeking a Byzantine–Mongol alliance (never realized) with Abaqa's grandson Öljeitu (r. 1304–16) against Osman, founder of the line of Ottoman sultans. Meanwhile, sometime in the first decade of the fourteenth century, Maria took vows as a nun under the name Melania. As a patron of the Chora monastery (today Kariye Mosque in Istanbul), her donor portrait appears in a mosaic depicting Christ and the Virgin (the Deësis) with the inscription 'the Lady of the Mongols, Melane the nun' (illus. 57). Most famously, she founded a monastery dedicated to Mary as the Holy Mother of God, informally known in her honour as Saint Mary of the Mongols (illus. 58) – the only church dating from the Byzantine period to have remained Christian to this day.

Conclusion

Born a decade or so after the historical figures we have explored in this chapter, the great Italian poet Dante Alighieri (1265–1321) completed *Paradiso*, the third part of his *Divine Comedy*, in about 1320. In some oft-quoted lines in Canto XIX, Dante wrestles with the question of the (in)justice of how 'a man born/ on the banks of the Indus, with no one there/ who speaks, or reads, or writes about Christ' and dies 'unbaptized and without faith' can be condemned, even though he led a sinless life.[30] In response, his guide and interlocutor, the Roman poet Virgil, reprimands him for thinking that human reason could comprehend God's judgement. In a Latin European context, Dante's anguish over the fate of unbaptized Indians was progressive for his time. But over two decades earlier, as we have seen, Marco Polo had described 'Yogi' who 'go about completely naked', 'worship cattle' and anoint their bodies with powdered cow dung (§177, p. 167) with total equanimity. This comparison with the writings of his own younger contemporary underscores the extraordinary capaciousness of Marco's world view – nurtured, without a doubt, by the mercantile practicality first evinced by his father and uncle, combined with his intimate familiarity with the diversity and complexity of the world. Marco had arrived at the Mongol court in the mid-1270s and gained the favour of the Great Khan, much as Zhao Mengfu would do over a dozen years later. In the early 1290s, Marco – still in the company of his father Niccolò and his uncle Maffeo – returned to Venice, stopping at the coastal Indian ports to the south of Amīr Khusrau's Delhi sultanate and traversing the Ilkhanate, on the traces of Despina Khatun, the Byzantine princess Maria Palaiologina.

Afterword

All of you who wish to know the diverse races of men and the diversities of the diverse regions of the world, take this book and have it read. Here you will find all the greatest marvels and great diversities of Greater Armenia, Persia, the Tartars, India, and many other provinces, as our book will tell you clearly, in orderly fashion, just as Messer Marco Polo, wise and noble citizen of Venice, tells because he saw it with his own eyes.

Description §1, p. 1

Marco Polo died in 1324 having lived an eventful life of seventy years that included not only his long sojourn in Asia but his captivity in Genoa and his fortuitous collaboration with Rustichello of Pisa. In the year following Marco's death, the young Moroccan scholar Ibn Battuta set out on what would eventually prove to be an even longer period of travels to East Africa, the Middle East and Asia, earning him the distinction of the Middle Ages' greatest long-distance traveller. By the time he returned to his home in Tangiers in 1354, however, the world had been irrevocably reshaped by the Black Death that swept from Central Asia throughout Europe near mid-century, occasioning demographic and social changes that now conventionally serve to demarcate the 'high' from the 'late' Middle Ages.

In the meantime, the Mongol century was coming to an end. The Ilkhanate of Persia fell in the 1330s, followed by Yuan China in 1368. This was the world that Marco Polo chronicled in the *Description*, and whose 'greatest marvels and great diversities' this book's pages have aimed to bring to life.

CHRONOLOGY

1294	Qubilai Khan dies.
	Genoese win a naval victory over the Venetians near Ayas
1295	The Polos return to Venice
1296	Zhao Mengfu, *Horse and Groom* and *Man Riding*
1298	Marco Polo and Rustichello of Pisa compose *The Description of the World*.
	Battle of Curzola: Genoese naval victory over Venice
1310	BNF MS Français 1116 (the 'F' text) copied
1321	Martyrdom of four Franciscan missionaries in Tana (West Indian coast)
1324	Marco Polo dies
1335	Ilkhanids overthrown in Persia
1336	British Library Royal MS 19 D 1 (*The Book of the Great Khan*) made for Philip VI
1348	Beginning of the Black Death in Europe
1368	Yuan dynasty overthrown by the Ming in China
1402	Battle of Ankara: Timur the Lame defeats the Ottomans
c. 1410	BNF MS Français 2810 (*The Book of Marvels*) produced
1532	Marco's text repackaged as a travel narrative ('Of Eastern Lands') in the Latin print compilation *Novus Orbis*
1559	Marco's text appears in Ramusio's Italian print translation

REFERENCES

Introduction

1 David Jacoby, 'Marco Polo, His Close Relatives, and His Travel Account: Some New Insights', *Mediterranean Historical Review*, XXI/2 (2006), pp. 193–218.
2 Martin da Canal, *Les Estoires de Venise*, trans. Laura K. Morreale (Padua, 2009), p. 3.
3 Throughout, references to and citations from Marco Polo's book are keyed to Marco Polo, *The Description of the World*, trans. Sharon Kinoshita (Indianapolis, IN, 2016), which also contains a series of maps and genealogical tables.
4 Frances Wood, *Did Marco Polo Go to China?* (Boulder, CO, 1996), p. 154.

1 Marco Polo and His World

1 Simon Gaunt, *Marco Polo's Le Devisement du Monde: Narrative Voice, Language and Diversity* (Cambridge, 2013).
2 Brunetto Latini, *The Book of the Treasure (Li livres dou trésor)*, trans. Paul Barrette and Spurgeon Baldwin (New York, 1993), I.121, pp. 85–6.
3 C. E. Beneš, ed. and trans., *Jacopo da Varagine's Chronicle of the City of Genoa* (Manchester, 2020), pp. 92–3.
4 Martin da Canal, *Les Estoires de Venise*, trans. Laura K. Morreale (Padua, 2009), pp. 3–4.
5 Olivia Remie Constable, *Housing the Stranger in the Mediterranean World: Lodging, Trade, and Travel in Late Antiquity and the Middle Ages* (Cambridge, 2003), p. 123.
6 Da Canal, *Les Estoires*, p. 95.
7 Idrîsî, *La première géographie de l'Occident*, trans. Annliese Nef (Paris, 1999), p. 372 (my translation from the French).
8 Keith Devlin, *The Man of Numbers: Fibonacci's Arithmetic Revolution* (New York, 2011), p. 44.
9 Djamil Aissani and Dominique Valérian, 'Mathématiques, commerce et société à Béjaïa (Bugia) au moment du séjour de

Leonardo Fibonacci (xiie-xiiie siècles)', *Bolletino di Storia delle Scienze Matematiche*, xxiii/2 (2003), pp. 9–31 (at pp. 24, 26–7).

10 Cited in Steven A. Epstein, *Genoa and the Genoese, 958–1528* (Chapel Hill, nc, 1996), p. 166.

11 Idrîsî, *La première géographie*, pp. 371–2 (my translation of the French translation from the Arabic).

12 Beneš, *Jacopo da Varagine*, p. 88.

13 Ibid., p. 244.

14 Rabban Sawma, *The Monks of Kublai Khan, Emperor of China: Medieval Travels from China through Central Asia to Persia and Beyond (The History of Yahballaha iii)*, trans. Sir E. A. Wallis Budge (London, 2014), p. 181.

15 Beneš, *Jacopo da Varagine*, pp. 202–4.

16 Ibid., p. 70.

17 Ibid., p. 257.

18 Thomas T. Allsen, 'The Rasûlid Hexaglot in its Eurasian Cultural Context', in *The King's Dictionary. The Rasûlid Hexaglot: Fourteenth Century Vocabularies in Arabic, Persian, Turkic, Greek, Armenian and Mongol*, ed. Peter B. Golden (Leiden, 2000), pp. 25–48 (p. 29).

19 Vladimir Drimba, ed., *Codex Comanicus: édition diplomatique avec fac-similés* (Bucharest, 2000), pp. 35–109.

20 Fabrizio Cigni, 'Copisti prigionieri (Genova, fine sec. xiii)', *Studi di Filologia romanza offerti a Valeria Bertolucci Pizzorusso*, 2 vols, ed. Pietro G. Belgrami et al. (Pisa, 2007), vol. i, pp. 425–39 (p. 436).

2 The Book of the Great Khan

1 Jonathan Chaves, trans. and ed., *The Columbia Book of Later Chinese Poetry: Yüan, Ming, and Ch'ing Dynasties (1279–1911)* (New York, 1986), pp. 27–8.

2 J. A. Giles, trans., *Matthew Paris's English History From the Year 1235 to 1273*, vol. i (London, 1852), p. 131.

3 Christopher Dawson, trans., *Mission to Asia*, 2nd revd edn (Toronto, 1980), p. 32.

4 Peter Jackson, trans., *The Mission of Friar William of Rubruck: His Journey to the Court of the Great Khan Möngke, 1253–1255* (Indianapolis, in, 2009), p. 74.

5 Christopher P. Atwood, trans., *The Secret History of the Mongols* (London, 2023), p. 158.

6 Thomas T. Allsen, *The Steppe and the Sea: Pearls in the Mongol Empire* (Philadelphia, pa, 2019), p. 151.

7 Ibid.

8 Jameel and Hilcia, 'Hangzhou – Venice of the East', Local Yet Not, 16 March 2017, www.localyetnot.com, accessed 22 June 2022.

9 Cited in Heng Chye Kiang, *Cities of Aristocrats and Bureaucrats: The Development of Medieval Chinese Cityscapes* (Honolulu, HI, 1999), pp. 106–7.

10 Xiaolin Duan, 'The Ten Views of Westlake', in *Visual and Material Cultures in Middle Period China*, ed. Patricia Buckley Ebrey and Shih-Shan Susan Huang (Leiden, 2017), pp. 151–89 (p. 154).

11 Christian de Pee, 'Nature's Capital: The City as Garden in *The Splendid Scenery of the Capital (Ducheng jisheng, 1235)*', in *Senses of the City: Perceptions of Hangzhou and Southern Song China, 1127–1279*, ed. Joseph S. C. Lam et al. (Hong Kong, 2017), pp. 179–204 (p. 179).

3 The Book of Marvels

1 John Larner, *Marco Polo and the Discovery of the World* (New Haven, CT, 1999), pp. 107–8.

2 The J. Paul Getty Museum Collection, MS Ludwig XV 4 (83.MR.174), www.getty.edu/art/collection/objects/1437, accessed 27 October 2023.

3 C. E. Beneš, ed. and trans., *Jacopo da Varagine's Chronicle of the City of Genoa* (Manchester, 2020), pp. 233–4, 249–50.

4 Eamon Duffy, 'Introduction to the 2012 Edition', in Jacobus de Voragine, *The Golden Legend: Readings on the Saints*, trans. William Granger Ryan (Princeton, NJ, 2012), pp. xi–xxi.

5 Jacobus de Voragine, *Golden Legend*, pp. 29–35.

6 Ibid., p. 35.

7 Brunetto Latini, *The Book of the Treasure (Li livres dou trésor)*, trans. Paul Barrette and Spurgeon Baldwin (New York, 1993), 1.75 (p. 43).

8 For example, Peter Jackson, trans., *The Mission of Friar William of Rubruck: His Journey to the Court of the Great Khan Möngke, 1253–1255* (Indianapolis, IN, 2009), pp. 163–4.

9 John Andrew Boyle, trans., 'Alā al-Dīn 'Aṭā Malik Juvaynī, *The History of the World-Conqueror* (Cambridge, MA, 1958).

10 Joseph de Somogyi, 'A *Qasīda* on the Destruction of Baghdād by the Mongols', *Bulletin of the School of Oriental Studies*, VII/1 (1933), pp. 41–8 (at 45, l.3).

11 Latini, *Book of the Treasure*, 1.122 (p. 90).

12 Captain Buzurg ibn Shahriyar of Ramhormuz, *The Book of the Wonders of India: Mainland, Sea and Islands*, ed. and trans. G.S.P.

Freeman-Grenville (London, 1981); Garden §86, pp. 77–8; Sea voyages §§90–91, pp. 80–83.

13 Compare *Book of the Wonders* §77, p. 73 and *Description* §169, p. 154.

14 Sharon Kinoshita, 'Traveling Texts: De-Orientalizing Marco Polo's *The Description of the World*', in *Travel, Agency, and the Circulation of Knowledge*, ed. Gesa Mackenthun, Andrea Nicolas and Stephanie Wodianka (Münster, 2017), pp. 223–46 (at pp. 238–40).

4 Animal, Vegetable, Mineral: Merchants and Their World

1 François-Xavier Fauvelle, *The Golden Rhinoceros: Histories of the African Middle Ages*, trans. Troy Tice (Princeton, NJ, 2018), p. 6.

2 William of Adam, *How to Defeat the Saracens: Guillelmus Ade, Tractatus quomodo Sarraceni sunt expungnandi*, ed. and trans. Giles Constable et al. (Washington, DC, 2012), pp. 99–101 (emphasis added).

3 Abū Zayd al-Sirāfī, *Accounts of China and India*, trans. Tim Mackintosh-Smith, Library of Arabic Literature (New York, 2017), §2.15.3, p. 64.

4 Ibid., §2.16.1, p. 65.

5 Charles Perry, ed. and trans., *Scents and Flavors: A Syrian Cookbook* (New York, 2017), §1.3, p. 7.

6 Cameron Cross, *Love at a Crux: The New Persian Romance in a Global Middle Ages* (Toronto, 2023), p. 94.

7 Joinville and Villehardouin, *Chronicles of the Crusades*, trans. Caroline Smith (London, 2008), p. 192.

8 Pliny, *Natural History*, vol. IV: *Libri XIII–XVI*, trans. H. Rackham (Cambridge, MA, 1945), p. 21 (my modification from 'pungency' to 'bitterness' (*amaritudine*)). Pliny elsewhere inveighed against the fashion for imported silk.

9 Shihab al-Din al-Nuwayri, *The Ultimate Ambition in the Arts of Erudition: A Compendium of Knowledge from the Classical Islamic World*, ed. and trans. Elias Muhanna (New York, 2016), p. 209.

10 Perry, *Scents and Flavors*, §§10–14, p. 269.

11 al-Nuwayri, *Ultimate Ambition*, p. 210.

12 Perry, *Scents and Flavors*, §5.58, p. 67.

13 Chau Ju-Kua, *On the Chinese and Arab Trade*, ed. and trans. Friedrich Hirth and W. W. Rockhill (Amsterdam, 1966), p. 193.

14 al-Nuwayri, *Ultimate Ambition*, p. 43. The subsection also surveys phenomena as varied as intellectual and professional qualities, jewels, clothing, furs, horses, poisonous animals, sweets, fruits,

aromatic plants, the physical features and manners of different
peoples, illnesses and meteorological phenomena.

15 Captain Buzurg ibn Shahriyar of Ramhormuz, *The Book of the
Wonders of India: Mainland, Sea and Islands*, ed. and trans. G.S.P.
Freeman-Grenville (London, 1981), p. 106.
16 Paul Freedman, *Out of the East: Spices and the Medieval Imagination*
(New Haven, CT, 2008), pp. 135–6.
17 al-Sirāfī, *Accounts of China and India*, §1.8.3, p. 17.
18 Suzanne G. Valenstein, *A Handbook of Chinese Ceramics*, revd and
enl. edn (New York, 1989), p. 99.
19 al-Nuwayri, *Ultimate Ambition*, p. 41.

5 Portrait Gallery: Marco Polo's Contemporaries

1 Shane McCausland, *Zhao Mengfu: Calligraphy and Painting for
Khubilai's China* (Hong Kong, 2011), pp. 14, 340–41.
2 Ibid., p. 214.
3 Ibid., p. 218.
4 Patricia Buckley Ebrey, ed., 'A Scholar-Painter's Diary', trans. Clara
Yu, in *Chinese Civilization: A Sourcebook*, 2nd edn (New York,
1993), pp. 199–201.
5 Zhou Mi, *Record of Clouds and Mist Passing Before One's Eyes*,
ed. and trans. Ankeney Weitz (Leiden, 2002), pp. 176–82;
McCausland, *Zhou Mengfu*, pp. 58–61. The *Record* also includes
an entry on Zhao's father, Zhao Yuyin, who had died in 1265
(indicating that Zhou had been compiling his catalogue for years).
Zhou Mi, *Record of Clouds and Mist*, pp. 190–92.
6 Zhou Mi, *Record of Clouds and Mist*, p. 220.
7 Marsha Weidner et al., *Views from Jade Terrace: Chinese Women
Artists, 1300–1912* (Indianapolis, IN, 1988), p. 66.
8 Ibid.
9 Ibid., p. 66, but note the complexities of dating the colophon and
the identity of its author (see p. 68, n.1).
10 Ibid., p. 67.
11 McCausland, *Zhao Mengfu*, pp. 344, 364–5.
12 Jennifer Purtle, 'Guan Daosheng and the Idea of a Great Woman
Artist', *Orientations*, XLIX/2 (2018), p. 9.
13 McCausland, *Zhao Mengfu*, pp. 105, 327–9, 359, 369–70.
14 Paul E. Losensky and Sunil Sharma, trans. and intro., 'Introduction',
in *In the Bazaar of Love: The Selected Poetry of Amir Khusrau* (New
Delhi, 2011), pp. xxiv–xxv.

15 R. Nath and Faiyaz Gwaliari, trans., *India as Seen by Amir Khusrau (in 1318 A.D.)* (Jaipur, 1981), p. 4, citing Muhammad Wahid Mirza, *The Life and Works of Amir Khusrau* (Calcutta, 1935), p. 20. The *ghazal* is a short lyric, typically on the topic of love, that became immensely popular (particularly in Sufi circles) in twelfth- and thirteenth-century Persian.

16 Richard M. Eaton, *India in the Persianate Age, 1000–1765* (Oakland, CA, 2019), pp. 55–6.

17 See Paul Smith, trans., *Divan of Amir Khusrau* (Campbells Creek, Victoria, 2018) and Losensky and Sharma, *Bazaar of Love*.

18 Nath and Gwaliari, *India as Seen by Amir Khusrau*, pp. 26 (III.8) and 28 (III.32).

19 Ibid., pp. 39, 49, 82–3.

20 Ibid., pp. 55, 59–60.

21 Ibid., pp. 97–100.

22 Ibid., pp. 69–72.

23 Ibid., pp. 70–71.

24 Ibid., p. 70.

25 Martin da Canal, *Les Estoires de Venise*, trans. Laura K. Morreale (Padua, 2009), p. 3.

26 Ibid., pp. 57, 72, 75–6. See also *The Description of the World*, §§180, 182–8.

27 Losensky and Sharma, *Bazaar of Love*, pp. xxxi–xxxiii, 114.

28 Ibid., pp. 98–9.

29 Eaton, *India in the Persianate Age*, pp. 66–70; Sunil Sharma, trans.,'Biographical Account of Amir Khusraw from Amir Khurd's *Siyar al-awliya*', in *Amir Khusraw: The Poet of Sultans and Sufis* (Oxford, 2005), pp. 93–8.

30 Dante Alighieri, *Paradiso*, trans. Stanley Lombardo (Indianapolis, IN, 2017), XIX, lines 70–72, p. 76.

BIBLIOGRAPHY

Abu-Lughod, Janet L., *Before European Hegemony: The World
   System, AD 1250–1350* (New York, 1989). A classic study
   of the unprecedented interconnectivity of Eurasia resulting
   from the Mongol conquests
Allsen, Thomas, *Commodity and Exchange in the Mongol Empire:
   A Cultural History of Islamic Textiles* (Cambridge, 1997).
   A major work shifting the emphasis from political and military
   history to the Mongols' considerable economic and cultural
   accomplishments, centred on the production and trade in textiles
—, *Culture and Conquest in Mongol Eurasia* (Cambridge, 2001)
—, *The Steppe and the Sea: Pearls in the Mongol Empire* (Philadelphia,
   PA, 2019)
Atwood, Christopher P., trans., *The Rise of the Mongols: Five Chinese
   Sources* (Indianapolis, IN, 2021). Primary texts documenting early
   Chinese reactions to and interactions with the Mongols, prefaced
   by a lengthy introduction of Chinese culture and conventions
—, trans., *The Secret History of the Mongols* (London, 2023). An
   accessible translation, by a noted scholar of the Mongols and China,
   of a Mongolian source chronicling the rise of Chinggis Khan in a
   vivid combination of prose, verse and dialogue. The introduction
   includes a masterful overview of Central Asian nomadic culture
   and practices
Barker, Hannah, *That Most Precious Merchandise: The Mediterranean
   Trade in Black Sea Slaves, 1260–1500* (Philadelphia, PA, 2019).
   A ground-breaking exploration of the trade in which the Genoese
   played a major role
Beneš, Carrie E., ed., *A Companion to Medieval Genoa*, Brill's
   Companions to European History 15 (Boston, MA, 2018).
   A comprehensive interdisciplinary collection. For material
   relating to our Chapter One, see in particular George L. Gorse,
   'Architecture and Urban Topography' (pp. 218–42); Rebecca
   Müller, 'Visual Culture and Artistic Exchange' (pp. 293–319);
   and Jeffrey Miner and Stefan Stantchev, 'The Genoese Economy'
   (pp. 397–426)

Berlekamp, Persis, *Wonder, Image, and Cosmos in Medieval Islam* (New Haven, CT, 2011). An art historian's study of the evolving tradition of al-Qazwīnī's *The Wonders of Creation*

Biran, Michal, Jonathan Brack and Francesca Fiaschetti, eds, *Along the Silk Roads in Mongol Eurasia: Generals, Merchants, and Intellectuals* (Oakland, CA, 2020)

Biran, Michal, and Hodong Kim, eds, *The Cambridge History of the Mongol Empire* (Cambridge, 2023)

Brook, Timothy, *The Troubled Empire: China in the Yuan and Ming Dynasties* (Cambridge, MA, 2010). Where traditional overviews tend to treat the Mongol Yuan dynasty as a kind of interregnum in the long history of China – or to group it with the preceding Liao and Jin dynasties as a period of alien rule – Brook's volume in Belknap Press's series on the History of Imperial China emphasizes some of the connections and continuities between the Yuan and the dynasty that succeeded it, the Ming

Bynum, Caroline Walker, 'Wonder', *American Historical Review*, CII/1 (1997), pp. 1–26. A noted cultural historian focuses on wonder as a key phenomenon in the medieval West

Constable, Olivia Remie, *Housing the Stranger in the Mediterranean World: Lodging, Trade, and Travel in Late Antiquity and the Middle Ages* (Cambridge, 2003)

Cruse, Mark, 'Novelty and Diversity in Illustrations of Marco Polo's *Description of the World*', in *Toward a Global Middle Ages: Encountering the World through Illuminated Manuscripts*, ed. Bryan C. Keene (Los Angeles, CA, 2019), pp. 195–202. An overview of the different visual programmes accompanying Marco Polo's text

Daston, Lorraine, and Katharine Park, *Wonders and the Order of Nature, 1150–1750* (New York, 1998). A philosophically and scientifically based history of wonders in the Western tradition

Eastmond, Antony, *Tamta's World: The Life and Encounters of a Medieval Noblewoman from the Middle East to Mongolia* (Cambridge, 2017)

Epstein, Steven A., *Genoa and the Genoese, 958–1528* (Chapel Hill, NC, 1996). The history of Genoa, one of the four maritime republics of medieval Italy, where *The Description of the World* was composed

——, *Speaking of Slavery: Color, Ethnicity, and Human Bondage in Italy* (Ithaca, NY, 2001)

——, *The Talents of Jacopo da Varagine: A Genoese Mind in Medieval Europe* (Ithaca, NY, 2016). A study of various writings of the archbishop of Genoa at the time Marco Polo was a captive there

Favereau, Marie, *The Horde: How the Mongols Changed the World*
(Cambridge, MA, 2021). A detailed study of the khanate commonly
known as the Golden Horde that offers expansive insights into
the Mongols' transition from steppe nomads to rulers of empire
Franke, Herbert, and Denis Twitchett, eds, *The Cambridge History
of China*, vol. VI: *Alien Regimes and Border States, 907–1368*
(Cambridge, 1994)
Freedman, Paul, *Out of the East: Spices and the Medieval Imagination*
(New Haven, CT, 2008)
Gadrat-Ouerfelli, Christine, *Lire Marco Polo au Moyen Âge: Traduction,
diffusion et réception du Devisement du monde* (Turnhout, 2015).
A complete catalogue of all known manuscripts of Marco Polo's text
Gaunt, Simon, *Marco Polo's Le Devisement du Monde: Narrative Voice,
Language and Diversity* (Cambridge, 2013). A noted scholar of Old
French argues for the primacy of the 'F' manuscript, underscoring its
emphasis on diversity
Herlihy, David, *Pisa in the Early Renaissance: A Study of Urban Growth*
(New Haven, CT, 1958). Study of the history of Rustichello's
hometown
Hilsdale, Cecily J., 'The Imperial Image at the End of Exile:
The Byzantine Embroidered Silk in Genoa and the Treaty
of Nymphaion (1261)', *Dumbarton Oaks Papers*, 64 (2010),
pp. 151–99. A spectacular example of the importance of gifts
and material objects in medieval diplomacy and power politics
Howard, Deborah, *Venice and the East: The Impact of the Islamic World
on Venetian Architecture, 1100–1500* (New Haven, CT, 2002).
An exploration of the way the Venetian built environment
intentionally celebrated its connection to the eastern
Mediterranean and the Islamic world
Jacoby, David, 'Marco Polo, His Close Relatives, and His Travel
Account: Some New Insights', *Mediterranean Historical Review*, XXI/2
(2006), pp. 193–218
Karnes, Michelle, *Medieval Marvels and Fictions in the Latin West and
Islamic World* (Chicago, IL, 2022)
Kinoshita, Sharon, 'Introduction', in Marco Polo, *The Description of the
World*, trans. Sharon Kinoshita (Indianapolis, IN, 2016), pp. xiv–xxv
—, 'Marco Polo and the Multilingual Middle Ages', in *Medieval
French Interlocutions: Shifting Perspectives on a Language in Contact*,
ed. Thomas O'Donnell, Jane Gilbert and Brian Reilly (York,
forthcoming). A look at some of the major languages across
thirteenth-century Eurasia

—, 'Sheep, Elephants and Marco Polo's *Devisement du monde*', in
   The Futures of Medieval French: Essays in Honour of Sarah Kay,
   ed. Jane Gilbert and Miranda Griffin (Woodbridge, 2021),
   pp. 314–27. A comparison of the representations and uses of
   two iconic animals in Eastern and Western cultures

—, 'Silk in the Age of Marco Polo', in *Founding Feminisms in Medieval
   Studies: Essays in Honor of E. Jane Burns*, ed. Laine E. Doggett
   and Daniel E. O'Sullivan (Cambridge, 2016), pp. 141–51

—, 'Traveling Texts: De-Orientalizing Marco Polo's *The Description
   of the World*', in *Travel, Agency, and the Circulation of Knowledge*,
   ed. Gesa Mackenthun, Andrea Nicolas and Stephanie Wodianka
   (Münster, 2017), pp. 223–46. A consideration of both academic and
   popular clichés on Marco Polo

Komaroff, Linda, and Stefano Carboni, eds, *The Legacy of Genghis Khan:
   Courtly Art and Culture in Western Asia, 1256–1353* (New York,
   2002). Lavishly illustrated catalogue of a 2002 special exhibit on
   the arts of Ilkhanate (Mongol-ruled Persia) at the Metropolitan
   Museum of Art

Lambourn, Elizabeth, 'Towards a Connected History of Equine Cultures
   in South Asia: *Bahrī* (Sea) Horses and "Horsemania" in Thirteenth-
   Century South India', *The Medieval Globe*, II/1 (2016), pp. 57–100.
   On the Indian Ocean trade in horses

Lane, Frederic C., *Venice: A Maritime Republic* (Baltimore, MD, 1973).
   Classic study of medieval and early modern Venice

Larner, John, *Marco Polo and the Discovery of the World* (New Haven, CT,
   1999). A classic introduction, including the later medieval history
   of the book

McCausland, Shane, *Zhao Mengfu: Calligraphy and Painting for Khubilai's
   China* (Hong Kong, 2011). A magisterial reassessment of the life and
   multivalent accomplishments of one of China's most important artists

Maguire, Henry, and Robert S. Nelson, eds, *San Marco, Byzantium,
   and the Myths of Venice* (Washington, DC, 2010). A collection of
   essays by art and architectural historians examining the ideological
   programmes behind Venice's built environment

Mathews, Karen Rose, 'Other Peoples' Dishes: Islamic Bacini on
   Eleventh-Century Churches in Pisa', *Gesta*, LIII/1 (2014),
   pp. 5–23. An examination of Pisa's distinctive way of showcasing
   its connections in the Islamic Mediterranean

—, Silvia Orvietani Busch and Stefano Bruni, eds, *A Companion to
   Medieval Pisa*, Brill's Companions to European History 28 (Leiden,
   2022)

May, Timothy, and Michael Hope, eds, *The Mongol World* (Abingdon, 2022). A magisterial collection of 58 essays valuably updating our knowledge of the Mongol world. In addition to political, military and economic histories, notable contributions include sections on Archaeology and Art History, The Mongols in the Eyes of the Conquered, Beyond the Borders of the Mongol Empire and The Mongol Legacy

Morgan, David O., *The Mongols,* 2nd edn (Malden, MA, 2007). A classic handbook on the Mongols

Perry, David M., *Sacred Plunder: Venice and the Aftermath of the Fourth Crusade* (University Park, PA, 2015). A study of the role of stolen objects in the construction of Venetian civic identity

Prange, Sebastian R., *Monsoon Islam: Trade and Faith on the Medieval Malabar Coast* (Cambridge, 2018). A history of the role of the spice trade, especially in pepper, in the Islamicization of the southwest Indian subcontinent

Rossabi, Morris, *Khubilai Khan: His Life and Times* (Berkeley, CA, 1988). The classic biography of Qubilai Khan

Shea, Eiren L., *Mongol Court Dress, Identity Formation, and Global Exchange* (New York, 2020). An art historian's reconstruction of Mongol clothing, based on a combination of surviving garments, textual accounts and art-historical representations

Wardwell, Anne E., *Panni Tartarici: Eastern Islamic Silks Woven with Gold and Silver, 13th and 14th Centuries* (New York, 1989). A close look at 'Tartar cloth', the Mongol-produced luxury textile that took medieval Europe by storm

Whitfield, Susan, 'The Perils of Dichotomous Thinking: A Case of Ebb and Flow Rather than East and West', in *Marco Polo and the Encounter of East and West*, ed. Suzanne Conklin Akbari and Amilcare A. Iannucci (Toronto, 2008), pp. 247–61

Yamashita, Michael, *Marco Polo: A Photographer's Journey*, revd edn (Vercelli, 2002). A beautiful album of a *National Geographic* photographer's journey retracing Marco Polo's itinerary, emphasizing those landscapes and peoples still corresponding to his thirteenth-century account

Zadeh, Travis, *Wonders and Rarities: The Marvelous Book that Traveled the World and Mapped the Cosmos* (Cambridge, MA, 2023). A literary and cultural historian's study of al-Qazwīnī's *The Wonders of Creation*

ACKNOWLEDGEMENTS

In the more than fifteen years that I have been working on Marco Polo, I have benefited immensely from the generosity, advice and encouragement of many. This book is in many ways a companion piece to my annotated translation of *The Description of the World*. That project owes its existence to the late Simon Gaunt, whose study *Marco Polo's Le Devisement du Monde: Narrative Voice, Language and Diversity* (Cambridge, 2013) first convinced me of the necessity of a new and accessible translation of Marco Polo's text. Rick Todhunter at Hackett Press undertook and oversaw that project to completion and Chris Atwood's perspective as an expert on all things Mongol greatly enriched the final version of the translation in ways that continue to resonate in the present work.

Brian Catlos and the wonderful circle of scholars from our Mediterranean Seminar have provided an intellectual home that enriched my knowledge of the Mediterranean and West Asia in ways far surpassing my training as a French medievalist. Thanks to the many friends and colleagues whose invitations to deliver lectures or contribute to edited volumes led me to explore many different aspects of Marco Polo's work. My students at the University of California, Santa Cruz constituted the first audience for many of the angles on Marco Polo that I have developed in this book. Grants from the Academic Senate's Committee on Research at the University of California, Santa Cruz provided financial support. I especially thank Samantha Stringer for her superlative research assistance in the final stages of the project.

My thanks to Alex Ciobanu at Reaktion Books for his invaluable assistance with the images and to Sebastian Ballard for drawing the maps.

As always, I thank Will Crooke and Monique Young for their friendship, interest and support.

PHOTO ACKNOWLEDGEMENTS

The author and publishers wish to express their thanks to the sources listed below for illustrative material and/or permission to reproduce it. Some locations of artworks are also given below, in the interest of brevity:

Alamy Stock Photo: 19 (Massimo Piacentino), 58 (Shaun Higson/Istanbul); © S. Ballard 2023: 7, 13, 23, 30; Bayerische Staatsbibliothek, Munich: 36 (Cod. Arab. 464, fols. 10r–10v); Bibliothèque nationale de France, Paris: 2 (MS Français 1116, fols. 3v–4r), 5 (MS Français 2810, fol. 76v), 35 (MS Français 2810, fol. 3r), 38 (MS Français 2810, fol. 194v); Bodleian Library, University of Oxford: 4 (MS Bodl. 264, fol. 218r), 26 (MS Bodl. 264, fol. 239r); British Library, London: 3 (Royal MS 19 D I, fol. 61r), 6 (Add. MS 22797, fol. 99v), 25 (Royal MS 19 D I, fol. 58r), 37 (MS Or. 14140, fol. 101v); Freer Gallery of Art, National Museum of Asian Art, Smithsonian Institution, Washington, DC: 32, 53; Gallerie dell'Accademia, Venice: 11; courtesy Marcella Giorgio, from Graziella Berti and Marcella Giorgio, *Ceramiche con coperture vetrificate usate come 'bacini'* (Florence, 2011): 44, 45; Heritage Auctions, HA.com: 27; iStock.com: 14 (nstanev), 15 (lkonya), 57 (stigalenas); courtesy Liao Yu-Kai, from Shane McCausland, *The Mongol Century* (London, 2014): 29; The Metropolitan Museum of Art, New York: 41, 42, 43, 46, 50, 52; Musée Condé, Chantilly: 34 (MS 65, fol. 1v); Musée du Louvre, Paris: 21; Museo di Sant'Agostino, Genoa: 20; National Library of China, Beijing: 31; National Museum of China, Beijing: 33; National Palace Museum, Taipei: 1, 22, 24, 54, 55, 56; Osaka City Museum of Fine Arts: 48; The Palace Museum, Beijing: 47, 49, 51; Shutterstock.com: 39 (SuperPapero); Wikimedia Commons: 8 (photo Nino Barbieri, CC BY-SA 2.5), 9 (photo Dimitris Kamaras, CC BY 2.0), 10 (photo Jean-Pol Grandmont, CC BY 4.0), 12 (photo Wolfgang Moroder, CC BY-SA 3.0), 16 (photo Marikevanroon20, public domain), 17 (photo Giuseppe Capitano, CC BY-SA 4.0), 18 (photo Zairon, CC BY-SA 4.0), 28 (photo Gary Todd, public domain), 40 (Hispanic Society of America, New York, photo Marie-Lan Nguyen, CC BY 2.5).

INDEX

Illustration numbers are indicated by *italics*